DISCARD

MOBILIZING
—— THE ——
ARMY
— OF —

GOD

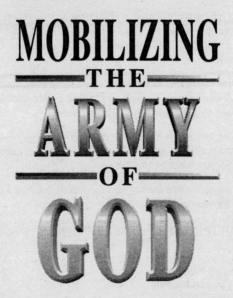

MOBILIZING
THE
ARMY
OF
GOD

RICK JOYNER

Whitaker House

MOBILIZING THE ARMY OF GOD

Rick Joyner
MorningStar Publications
16000 Lancaster Highway
Charlotte, NC 28277
1-800-542-0278

ISBN: 0-88368-376-8
Printed in the United States of America
Copyright © 1994 by Rick Joyner

Whitaker House
30 Hunt Valley Circle
New Kensington, PA 15068

4 5 6 7 8 9 10 11 12 / 05 04 03 02 01 00 99

Contents

Chapter Twelve

Chapter One

The Three Great Pillars

Church historians sometimes refer to the apostles Peter, Paul and John as the three pillars of the church. As we look from the perspective of church history, viewing Peter, Paul and John in this way gives us an interesting, and quite accurate, paradigm for interpreting our history.

Without question Peter, Paul and John had the greatest impact on the first century church. Peter actually laid the foundation with both the Jews and the Gentiles, but he was soon overshadowed by the extraordinary labors of Paul. Only after these two had entered into their reward as martyrs did John, with his mystical but profound revelation of his beloved Savior, ascend to the forefront of the church's emphasis. Interestingly, church history closely follows this same pattern.

The Nature Of Peter

Peter was impetuous, unstable, prone to both breathtaking victories and heartrending mistakes. At one point he was praised with one of the greatest honors the Lord ever gave to a man:

Blessed are you Simon Barjona, because flesh and blood did not reveal this to you, but My Father who is in heaven.

9

> **And I also say to you that you are Peter [a stone], and upon this rock [large rock—speaking on the revelation] I will build My church; and the gates of Hades shall not overpower it.**
>
> **I will give you the keys of the kingdom of heaven; and whatever you shall bind on earth shall be bound in heaven, and whatever you shall loose on earth shall be loosed in heaven (Matthew 16:17-19).**

Immediately after this greatest of affirmations Peter received possibly the greatest rebuke ever given to a man:

> **But He turned and said to Peter, "Get behind Me, Satan! You are a stumbling block to Me; for you are not setting your mind on God's interests, but man's" (Matthew 16:23).**

Peter was prone to the greatest of extremes. He received the greatest of commissions and the greatest of rebukes within the span of a couple of minutes! He would open the gates of heaven and then the gates of hell. He would walk on water and then deny the Lord. He would be the first to enter the home of a Gentile to preach the gospel, and then get so carried away in hypocrisy toward the Gentiles that the youngest of apostles would have to rebuke him publicly. The most spectacular successes would be quickly followed by the most devastating defeats. Peter was hot or cold—no one would ever accuse him of being lukewarm.

Peter: The First Pillar Of The Church

By the third century A.D., the developing church, with the notable exceptions of Tertullian and Augustine, began to almost completely ignore the Letters of Paul and the foundational principles that he had given to the church, as well as those of John, with his emphasis on relationship with the Lord. Peter became both the emphasis and the proclaimed seat upon which the Medieval church would sit.

Likewise, the nature of the church in the Middle Ages accurately parallels the nature of Peter. Spectacular victories would be followed by the adoption of some of the most diabolical errors. When studying the history of the church during this time we can almost hear the Lord saying repeatedly, "Blessed are you church," followed by, "Get behind Me, Satan!" Because Paul's letters were essentially ignored, all of the errors that Paul had spent his life standing against came flooding into the church during this period.

Peter was the evangelist par excellence. He boldly testified of the Lordship of Jesus, opening the door of faith to both the Jews and the Gentiles. The Medieval church also spread the fame of the Savior over the known world. The "conquests" of the church during this time were every bit as extraordinary in history as the ministry of Peter is in Scripture. Like Peter, the church was persecuted and sometimes "imprisoned," but she also would have miraculous escapes that led to even greater advances for the gospel. During this time the greatest real threat to the church was not the forces without, but those within. The serious errors that crept into the fabric of the church were far more threatening than any of the forces that were arrayed against the church from without.

Paul Again Rebukes Peter

In time the Reformation was born as Hus, Luther, Zwingli, Calvin and other powerful church leaders "rediscovered" the Pauline Epistles. The Reformation could be viewed somewhat as Paul again standing up to publicly rebuke Peter for his serious errors. Now, for over five hundred years the Protestant church has focused its attention mostly on the epistles and doctrines of Paul.

Paul, considered to be the greatest teacher in church history, was the greatest champion of the freedom that Jesus purchased for every believer. These foundational truths were recovered by The Reformation church, and she once again became the greatest source of truth the world has ever known. The Reformation churches became so committed to the value of individual faith that it actually gave birth to the democratic form of government. This emphasis was greatly needed and has unquestionably blessed the world. However, there is a third "pillar," and the transformation to this third great phase of the church has now begun.

The Final Phase Of Church History

Just as the apostle John did not come into his place as the prevailing influence until the other two great pillars of the church had passed, so it is again at the end that John will have the last word.

When John was called by Jesus he was mending nets (See Matthew 4:21), which was a fitting representation of his future purpose. His letters bound together and completed the message of the New Testament, just as the Book of Revelation bound together and completed the whole canon of Scripture. With his great revelation John was given the last word in canon Scripture, and so the "ministry" of this great pillar of the church will be the final message of this church age. Could this be what the Lord meant when He said to Peter concerning John, **"If I want him to remain until I come, what is that to you?" (John 21:22).** It does appear that it will be the message of John which will be prevailing in the church when the Lord comes.

Peter was the evangelist; Paul was the teacher; John was the prophet. John somehow remained aloof from the conflict between Jewish and Gentile Christianity, and the clashes between Paul and Peter. We must understand the importance of these conflicts and their proper resolution for all of Christianity, but John's vision was beyond doctrine—he was not just devoted to the words of the Lord, but to the Word Himself. John saw Him Who was the beginning, and then on the Isle of Patmos he saw Him who was the End—John knew the Alpha and the Omega.

The Ministry Of John

John was prophetic. The enemy has been successful in implanting a caricature of this ministry that is very different from its true nature. The commonly accepted concept of prophets is that they are angry and always looking for what is wrong with everyone else. However, John, who is probably the most perfect example of the true prophetic nature in the Age of Grace, was very different. His emphasis was on abiding in the Lord and loving one another. Nor was he dogmatic, but he was much more prone to view the great concepts of the faith than to be a stickler for doctrinal purity.

As Paul was especially in tune with the mind of Christ, John leaned his head upon the breast of the Lord where he could hear the heartbeat of God. This is the essence of the true prophetic ministry—intimacy with God. First and foremost this will be the greatest contribution of the prophetic ministry to the last day church. The place that John had, leaning upon His breast, is now available to anyone who desires it. The Scriptures clearly testify that we are all as close to the Lord as we want to be. If we draw near to Him He will draw near to us. The veil has been rent, and we can enter into His presence if we choose to.

Intimacy with God is the most contagious power on the face of the earth. Jesus is the true desire of every human heart. When He is lifted up by the church He will draw all men to Himself. The church now knows much and has done much for the sake of the gospel, but the last and greatest thing that we can do still remains, which is simply to become intimate with God. As we draw near to Him we will become like Him, and that is what the world is waiting to see. Until we live what we say, the world has an excuse not to believe our words.

The scope of John's vision lifted men into the spiritual realm. During his vision on the Isle of Patmos, John saw Babylon from the valley, but when he was carried to a "high mountain" he saw the New Jerusalem. From the earthly perspective men will get caught up in the confusion and doctrinal conflicts of Babylon. When we are caught up into the heavenly places to see as God sees, we do not see the confusion and conflict in the church—we see what God is building.

To the earthbound and the visionless, the great doctrines like "free-will" and "election" conflict with each other, but from God's perspective they wonderfully compliment one another. John would have never been a Calvinist or an Armenian, but could have had great fellowship with each, and would have drawn out the essence of their truths. Neither would John have been a Catholic, a Protestant, an Evangelical, a Pentecostal, a Charismatic or member of the Third, Fourth or Fifth Waves—but he would have loved every one of them.

John never succumbed to the carnality of doctrinal divisions. This was not because he did not care about truth, but because his vision was high enough to perceive the truth as it was, and one truth will never conflict with another truth. John did not see truths as just facts, but he saw Jesus as *the Truth*. John saw beyond the church—his vision was fastened upon the glorified Christ.

The Heartbeat Of God

Fittingly, it was John who recorded in his gospel the last great prayer of Jesus before He entered into His passion. When facing death the ultimate issues of the heart are revealed. It was on this last night that the heart of Jesus was so profoundly expressed in His prayer to the Father. In this situation Jesus prayed for that which He cared the most about—His church.

First He prayed, **"Sanctify them in the truth; Thy word is truth" (John 17:17).** To be sanctified in the truth involves more than just believing it; this requires that we be changed by it.

It is not believing in our minds, but with our hearts which results in righteousness (See Romans 10:10). When we begin to believe in our hearts what we believe in our minds, then our lives will be radically different, and our words will be ultimately powerful. Living waters only come out of the "innermost being," and our message will not be living until it comes from our hearts. It will be the prophetic ministry with John's nature that will help transform the great truths that have been deposited in the church from doctrine to a lifestyle. Only when they become life will they produce unity.

The Lord then prayed, "…**that they may all be one; even as Thou, Father, art in Me, and I in Thee, that they also may be in Us…**" **(verse 21).** This is not just agreement about doctrines, or even coming together around the same projects or visions. Jesus prayed for His church to have a unity of the most extraordinary kind— that we would have the same union with each other that He had with the Father!

This kind of unity can only come one way—by our receiving the very last thing that Jesus prayed for us to have: "… **that the love wherewith Thou didst love Me may be in them, and I in them**" **(verse 26).** This might be the greatest single thought contained in the Scripture— that we could actually have, abiding in us, the same love for Jesus that the Father had for Him!

It was also John who wrote: **"And this is the confidence which we have before Him, that, if we ask anything according to His will, He hears us. And if we know that He hears us in whatever we ask, we know that we have the requests which we have asked from Him"** **(I John 5:14-15).** Since we know that Jesus was of one mind with the Father, and that He only prayed according to His will, we can know by this that it is His will that we have in us the same love for His Son that He has. Is there anything greater than this that should be at the top of our prayer list?

This last request of the Son before His passion is the key to the fulfillment of His other requests. When we have the same love for Him that the Father has, we will be sanctified by the greatest truth in the universe—that

God is love and He wants us all to love His Son as intensely as He does. Such love would never do anything to injure or cause division within His church. Such love would remain pure just as the purest bride for the husband she adores.

The glory of God is much more than just golden light or brilliant colors. The true glory of God is revealed in His nature. In the ultimate sense the glory of God is best perceived in the love between the Father and the Son. The Holy Spirit is the personification of that love, and He exists to reveal this great love. When He moved upon "the formless void" it was to bring forth Jesus;

> **And he is the image of the invisible God, the first-born of all creation.**
>
> **For by Him all things were created, both in the heavens and on earth, visible and invisible, whether thrones or dominions or rulers or authorities—*all things have been created by Him and for Him*.**
>
> **And He is before all things, and *in Him all things hold together*.**
>
> **He is also head of the body, the church; and He is the beginning, the first-born from the dead; *so that He Himself might come to have first place in everything*.**
>
> ***For it was the Father's good pleasure for all the fullness to dwell in Him,***

and through Him to reconcile all things to Himself… (Colossians 1:15-20).

The Lord Jesus also prayed that "… *the glory* which Thou hast given Me I have given to them; *that they may be one, just as We are one*" (John 17:22). The glory of God is His nature, which is most perfectly personified in Jesus. He has given us Jesus to be *in us*, that we might be one. If the whole creation is "held together" in Him, how much more union should the church have, which is first and foremost the beginning of the "new creation" in Him?

John later stated this foundational truth: "but if we walk in the light as He Himself is in the light, we have fellowship with one another…" (I John 1:7). The word "fellowship" evolved from the phrase "two fellows in a ship," with the inference being that, since there were just two of them, they had to work together if they were to get to their destination. If we walk in the light, as Jesus is in the light, we will have fellowship. Those who break fellowship with the church are no longer dwelling in the light.

We Must Have All Three

Ecclesiastes 4:12 reads: "And if one can overpower him who is alone, two can resist him. A cord of three strands is not quickly torn apart." When the church was built around the single pillar of emphasis upon Peter, evil did easily overpower it. As emphasis upon Paul's ministry was regained the church did become much more stable. However, for the church to be properly built it must be built upon the proper Foundation, which is Jesus Himself, and around all three of these three great pillars of the faith.

When the church ceases to be evangelistic and to reach out to the world, the dying process has begun. If she does not combine evangelistic zeal with sound doctrine she will fall into devastating errors as the church of the Middle Ages did. However, if the church does not combine these two essentials with prophetic vision into the realm of the Spirit, and the devotion to personal intimacy with the Lord that John understood, a form of godliness that denies His power and His presence will be the result.

We must thank God for Peter and for Paul. If all of the disciples had been of the nature of John, it is unlikely that 3,000 new believers would have been added to the church on the Day of Pentecost, or that the Gentiles would have ever had the gospel preached to them. If it were not for Paul and his great devotion to truth and the essence of the New Covenant, it is possible that the church would have just been absorbed back into Judaism. But without the ministry of John we may have a large and glorious church, with everything in perfect order—except there would be no God! Jesus Himself is the example of what all of these ministries are like when properly combined with the perfect heart of the Shepherd.

The prophetic ministry represented by John has a special place during the end of this age. This is not because it is more important than the others, but because it plays a special role in preparing the bride for her coming King. The Lord is yearning for His bride to mature, and to come forth without "spot or wrinkle." Having no spot speaks of her purity; having no wrinkle speaks of her perpetual youthfulness. The emerging prophetic ministry will help prepare the church in both purity of life and intimacy with the Lord, which is the source of her youthful love for Him.

Every Birth Is Painful

In many ways, the process of travail and birth subjects babies to the greatest pressures they will ever experience in life. The emerging prophetic ministry likewise has gone through a bloody and painful birth. This is not unique; the restoration of every ministry to the church went through a similar process.

It is also the nature of Satan to try to destroy everything that God is bringing to birth as soon as it emerges from the womb, since at that time it is the most vulnerable (see Revelation 12:1-4). Immediately after the most difficult struggles of the birth process, every seed of God is usually subject to its greatest attack from Satan. This too has happened to the last day prophetic ministry, but the baby has survived and is now growing in wisdom and stature. It is the destiny of this ministry to rise in stature until the prophetic nature thrives in the church, and is properly joined with the pillars of evangelism and teaching.

Whether we like it, or want it, the prophetic ministry will soon reach its greatest height of influence and stature in the church since the apostle John was exiled to Patmos. The whole church will be transformed by this ministry as much as it was by the Reformation influence of the teachers. This will not take as long because we are coming to the end of the age. We are now closer to the birth of the age in which Christ will reign, and the contractions of travail have become both more intense and more frequent, just as they do with a woman in childbirth.

Signs Of The End

On the Day of Pentecost, Peter quoted Joel, citing the great signs that would indicate the last days. He spoke, **"… your sons and your daughters shall prophesy, and your young men shall see visions, and your old men shall dream dreams…"(Acts 2:17).** These revelation gifts will indeed be a prevailing influence in the last day church. However, we could not handle these gifts properly if they were not built upon the strong pillars of evangelism and sound teaching. We must not abandon its predecessors because the prophetic has come, but rather fasten ourselves more firmly to them. If we remove any one of these pillars, then the house will be unstable; if we remove two of them then it will surely collapse.

Most congregations that I have visited reflect the basic nature of their pastor. There will be a strong evangelistic burden in the congregation, if he is an evangelist. If the pastor is a strong teacher, then the congregation will be strong in doctrine and devotion to the word, but it will often be weak in evangelism. A prophetic pastor will yield a congregation given to the prophetic gifts and experiencing encounters with the Lord, but which may be weak in evangelism and teaching. The last day church will be strong in all three, with each emphasis properly relating to, and supporting the others. Like the rope of three cords, the house of three pillars will be the strongest of all.

The ministries of Peter, Paul and John may have had some conflicts, but they are not in conflict with each other. In fact, there must be union between them if there is to be a true Christlike ministry revealed through the church again. The time has come when the "ministry of John" will ascend to the place of significant influence in the church, which will be needed for a season until all of the ministries come into harmony. As they do, congregations, denominations, and movements that receive the proper balance of all three will grow closer together. Then the house of the Lord will grow strong, full of His glory, a Holy Temple prepared for His presence.

Chapter Two

The Four Winds Of The Earth

After this I saw four angels standing at the four corners of the earth, holding back the four winds of the earth, so that no wind should blow on the earth or on the sea or on any tree.

And I saw another angel ascending from the rising of the sun, having the seal of the living God; and he cried out with a loud voice to the four angels to whom it was granted to harm the earth and the sea,

saying, "Do not harm the earth or the sea of the trees, until we have sealed the bond-servants of our God on their foreheads" (Revelation 7:1-3).

A "paradigm" is a model that we use for perceiving, understanding and interpreting the world. For the Christian there is no other paradigm but the Bible. The Bible gives us all of the general knowledge that we need for understanding history, the present, and the future. Understanding the four primary sources of power, or the biblical "winds of the earth" that effect foundational shifts in civilization, can provide a "grid" or "paradigm" for understanding the general flow of both history, the present and the future.

In Scripture winds often represent forces of change. There are four great "winds" of the earth that have set the course of history, which are the foundational power bases of RELIGION, POLITICS, ECONOMICS and the MILITARY. Each of these power bases has been able to fundamentally impact world affairs. The dominance of any one of these for an extended period of time has provided such a significant shift in civilization that it has resulted in a new historical epoch. Viewing history and biblical prophecy in the light of these gives an important understanding to world events.

The period preceding the advent of Christ was dominated by Military power. This was the age of the conquerors. Christianity became the first religion to actually sweep across the world and begin to rival the Military power base for influencing civilization. By the fourth century A.D. the Roman Emperor Constantine rightly discerned that the power base of Religion would actually eclipse the Military power base in influence. Perceiving that he could not beat it, he joined it, and began to subject the empire to the authority of the church. (In the context of this chapter, the "Religious power base" is related to the institutions of Religion as distinguished from personal religious faith.)

As Religion asserted itself as the dominant power base during the Middle Ages, the Military became more a servant of Religion, both in the Christian West and Moslem East. With the rise of Politics as a main source of power in the 18th century, both the Military and Religious power bases became servants of the Political forces. With the rise of Economics as the main source of influence during the twentieth century, with the polarities of communism and capitalism vying for the dominant role, the Military, Religious and Political power bases all became servants of the Economic power base.

This is not a comment on what is right, but what has in fact happened. History is not quite as clean and fluid as the above paragraph might infer. There are always some exceptions, but it does reflect the general course of history. There have been periods when the Military power base would reassert its influence and become dominant for a short period during the time of the Religious, Political or Economic eras, at least in certain regions of the world. We can also see the Religious power base reasserting itself as the primary source of influence at times and in specific places, such as the recent Islamic fundamentalist revolution in Iran. In the former Soviet Union we have an interesting clash of the Political, Economic and Military power bases all seeking a dominant role, with the Religious influence also growing dramatically through a grassroots revival.

It is useless just to know what happened in history if we do not understand it, including how it affects us today and will affect us tomorrow. The church is called to be the primary source of this understanding—the Lord had a good reason for telling His people history in advance with prophecies that are filled with all of the keys to understanding. Our understanding of our present place in prophecy, and the unfolding of the future, must be built on a solid foundation of knowing what has already been fulfilled, and why.

The Two Sources Of Winds

That the above power bases are called the "winds of the earth" and not winds of heaven indicate that these forces are of human origin, not divine. It is obvious that the Lord has also projected His own influence in history. Therefore, a true understanding of history requires that we be able to recognize and distinguish both the "winds of the earth" and "the winds of heaven."

The very word "history" is derived from combining the words "His" with "story" (i.e. the Lord's story). When John was given the Revelation on the Isle of Patmos, he was told that what he was about to be shown were **"the things which must shortly take place" (Revelation 1:1).** True to this statement, the events prophetically described in the vision immediately began to unfold and have continued to this day.

The failure of the church to understand history has been one of the fundamental reasons why she has also failed to properly understand the Book of Revelation. Even more importantly, this is a primary reason why the church has ceased to be a major factor in setting the course of history—but this is about to change. The church is called to be the vehicle of God's influence on earth in the last days, and to stand resolutely against the powers of this age. However, "we must box so as not to beat the air," which means we must know what we are fighting against.

The Man Of Sin

History really is "His-story." Also included in the Revelation, which was a history book written in advance, is a revelation of "the man of sin," or the "antichrist." This "man of sin" is a personification of the "sin of man." The man of sin is a revelation of what the fallen race of man is without Christ. A primary description of the man of sin's character is given by the apostle Paul in II Thessalonians 2:4: "... **he takes his seat in the temple of God, displaying himself as being God.**"

Self-worship, as personified in the "man of sin," is a fundamental characteristic of fallen mankind. The fall was caused by our wanting to be like God. Here we also see that the "man of sin" is not just against Christ, but is a *substitute for Christ*. This temple where he takes his seat is not a physical building, in Jerusalem or anywhere else—the temple of God is no longer one made with hands—it is the church! This prophecy that the man of sin takes his seat in the temple of God represents the fact that the most base representation of fallen man, or the sin of man, will actually sit in the church for a time and usurp Christ's rightful place. Jesus is the *only* true Head of the church.

The attention given to this man of sin in this vision of John's, which was given as "a revelation of Jesus Christ," is so that we can see the degree to which this terrible propensity toward self-worship has worked in man, and even in the church. This represents the ultimate apostasy. This is not to imply that the "man of sin" will not be a literal man, but if we are to be free of his deception we must recognize the degree to which the same spirit may be working in us as individuals and as the church. However, it also gives us a greater revelation of the grace of God that is revealed in Christ to deliver man from this terrible delusion. There will yet be a church without spot of wrinkle, which will be the pure, chaste bride of Christ.

The Root Of Apostasy

It is possible for us to trace most of the significant failures of the church and her leaders to this tendency to try to sit in the Lord's seat as the head of the church. Certainly the Lord has given authority for His ministries to exercise in the church, and in the world, but we have been tragically prone to fail to recognize the limits of the authority delegated to us. The presumption of going beyond our commission can be seen as the root cause of many, if not most, of the significant failures of the church. The rest are usually the result of overreacting to the failures of going too far and failing to walk in the authority given to us.

As we approach the end it is imperative that we get this right and understand the limits of our authority. This is so that we will not continue to fall to the presumption that always leads to self-worship, self-seeking and self-preservation in ministry, but also so that we can fully exercise all of the authority that we have been given with confidence.

Understanding the "four winds of the earth" can help us to understand the fundamental forces that have led to the significant events of human history, which are unfolding to bring this age to a conclusion. We may also begin to comprehend how they have influenced the church, and how, at times, they sought to eclipse Christ as the primary influence in the church. The Book of Revelation shows the parallels of human, satanic and divine influences in history to reveal sin, folly and the ultimate triumph of God over them. We must understand and be able to recognize all three of these influences in history, the present and the future, along with our own commission and destiny.

The Four Epochs Of History

Each of the four "winds of the earth" has dominated an important age in world history. The Empire Age, which dated basically from the beginning of recorded history until about the fourth century A.D., was essentially a Military age. During this period Military power as a primary tool of influence was developed and used.

From that point until the Renaissance the world was mostly controlled by the Religious power base, with institutional Christianity rising in the West and Islam in the East. Having already been developed, the Military was used as a tool of those seeking religious dominance. Both Politics and Economics were being developed during this time, but could not rival the influence of the Military or Religious power bases.

During the 17th century Politics began to emerge as a dominant force in world affairs. The Military and Religious power centers continued to operate, but mostly for exerting their influence for Political interests.

Politics, having developed gradually as a main power center, became a the primary power base in the 18th century, with alliances and political intrigue beginning to share, and then exert influence over the other developed bases of power. During this period Politics created the major impetus for wars, conflicts and conquests. At this time, new and sweeping changes in governments took place, such as the formation of democracy and socialism.

During the late 19th century Economics began to assert itself as the most powerful force in world affairs, and gradually gained dominion over the other three main power bases. Now Economics has become the primary power base and the primary power behind world affairs.

The Source Of The Beast's Power

It is important that we understand the ascension of these power bases and their present influence. Understanding that Economics is the primary driving force of world affairs at the end of the age helps us to understand how the beast seeks to gain dominance through commerce by controlling the "buying, selling and trading."

Revelation 13:16-17 teaches that the beast has a mark which he tries to place upon us. In chapter 14:9-10, we see that terrible wrath comes upon all who take the mark.

Christians have striven to understand the manner in which this beast would place his mark on them so that they would know what to refuse and be free of the wrath foretold. However, understanding how he places the mark is not as important as understanding the spiritual power behind the mark. Many of those who are frantically trying to understand how the beast will try to place his mark on them are already partaking of the spirit of the beast everyday! Will we be free of the curse of the mark if we refuse a physical mark but are, ourselves, of the very nature of the beast?

Just as the seal (literal "mark") that the Lord places upon His bondservants is not a physical mark, the mark of the beast is probably far more subtle than we have been led to believe. But regardless of the form in which the mark comes, or has come, those who have partaken of the nature of the beast, the spirit of the world, will not be able to resist the mark, or anything else from the beast. Our only deliverance from the wrath of God is to be found in Christ. Taking the mark is not a sin; the sin is found in worshipping the beast. The mark is merely the evidence of that worship.

As the world has generally been moving deeper into the period dominated by the Economic power base, we can observe that now most of the world-changing conflicts are economic in nature. The Cold War was a very real war, but it was an economic war not a military war. An Economic world war is now raging across the earth, changing Political and even Religious boundaries as much as any Military war ever did.

Clausewitz defined war as the Political extension of one nation's will over another. Clausewitz was a German officer during the Napoleonic wars and his book, *On War* interpreted war just as Machivalli's book *The Prince* had interpreted politics. Clausewitz lived during the time when the Political power base was preeminent, when human governments were being redefined and changed. In Clausewitz' time war truly was an extension of Politics. However, if Clausewitz were writing his classic book today he would almost certainly write that wars are basically extensions of Economic interests.

Understanding Economic War

The great clash between communism and capitalism was an Economic clash even more than it was a Political clash. The former Soviet Union was beaten Economically, not Militarily, or Politically. Just as religious power struggles often degenerated into Military wars during the Middle Ages, this could have happened during the Cold War, but by God's grace it did not. Even so, the Political and Economic changes that were accomplished by the Cold War were as sweeping and deep as have ever been accomplished during a Military war, including World War II.

The 1992 monetary crisis in Europe was the Economic equivalent of a significant military battle, only this battle was fought with banks and currencies instead of infantry and artillery. The long term effects of that monetary conflict promise to be as far reaching in their impact on the course of Europe as many of the great military battles fought between those same nations.

In the U.S. elections of 1992, President George Bush had the greatest backing of the Military, Religious, and even the major Political forces, but Bill Clinton beat him by perceiving that the Economic power base now has more influence than all of those combined. Again, this is not to imply what is right, or righteous, but what is in fact true. Economic power is now the greatest source of influence in the world, and the gap between this power and the others grows daily.

The War With Japan

It has been said often that the United States won the war against Japan but Japan has been winning the peace. The fact is that what we have been considering "peace" has been a very real war with every bit as much strategic significance as the World War fought with armies and navies. Japan may have surrendered the Military war, but it quickly declared Economic war on the United States. It will one day be understood that Japan has never been the friend of the United States, and it will try to pull economic strings that are designed to bring about the Economic ruin of the United States.

Many think that Japan would never try to do this because they now have too much invested in the U.S., but that is precisely why they now have so much invested in this country. Japan will one day drop major "Economic nuclear bombs" on the United States that are designed to bring about our surrender to their Economic powers.

Japan does understandably have a great deal of resentment toward the U.S. because of the nuclear bombs we dropped on them. However, they also greatly appreciate the grace with which the U.S. helped restore their nation. For the Japanese to supplant the U.S. as the world's greatest Economic power is not so much rooted in resentment, but in contempt for U.S. business leadership, coupled with their own fierce nationalism.

This is but one strategy through which Economic interests are seeking increasing dominion over the world. Understanding the present nature of this conflict is crucial for any nation that expects to field a successful "army" in this battle. The most important "generals" in this world war are corporate presidents, bankers and other economic leaders. The most important army is now composed of workers, small business owners, accountants and other business oriented professionals. Economic resources are now more important than bombs or bullets. Economic spying is now emphasized even more than military spying (It is interesting to note that the Soviets actually considered the IRS as the true counterparts of the KGB).

The Light And Salt

If the church is going to speak prophetically to her generation she must understand the signs of the times, which means that we must understand the times. These

four great "winds of the earth" were biblically antici-
pated and, to some degree, were shaped by divine inter-
vention at strategic times. Great revivals and
reformational influences certainly put their imprint on
each of the great sociological shifts in foundational
powers, and will have their greatest impact on the present
and impending sociological shifts.

Christians obviously had an important influence in the
development of the Religious epoch of human history.
Christianity was also a primary factor in the development
of Democracy, the greatest contribution of the Political
period's dominance of history. Christianity also had a
significant contribution to the development of free enterprise, the greatest contribution of the Economic period
of history. We can likewise observe satanic influences
countering the Christian influence in each of these periods. Even the best examples of democracy and free
enterprise still have doors that are open to evil influences,
and they will probably remain open until the King of
Kings returns to establish His dominion on the earth.
Even so, as the light of the world and salt of the earth,
the church has made great contributions to the development of human affairs, and we must continue to do so.
The evil one is obviously just as intent on establishing
his agenda for this period.

Neither the United States, nor any other country, is
presently the kingdom of God on earth. Revelation 11:15
states: **"And the seventh angel sounded; and there
arose loud voices in heaven, saying, 'The kingdom of
the world *has become* the kingdom of our Lord.'"**

This phrase "has become" implies that the kingdom of the world will make a *transition* to become the kingdom of God. It is obvious that the second coming of the Lord will be the climax of this change. Even so, this verse in Revelation, in its context, implies that there will be a transformation of the kingdom of the world prior to the second coming of the Lord, which has not yet come in the text of the Revelation. The world will not be totally evil when the Lord returns to set up His kingdom—there is actually a transformation now taking place that is laying the foundation for this change. We must also note that, in this text, the change comes *after* terrible cataclysmic events.

The great turmoil coming will represent the greatest time of trouble the world has ever known. By God's great grace, as we read in the opening text, He is going to give us a period of time in which He is going to hold back these "four great winds of the earth" so that His bondservants can be sealed. There will be a time of peace before the winds are released in the greatest conflicts of all. Then the winds of human power are going to blow like never before to sift the whole earth and all that man has built. That which is built upon the Rock, the ways of the Lord, will remain; everything else will be swept away.

How Should We Then Live?

We see that it is before this that the four angels are sent to hold back the "four winds of the earth" "… **until we have sealed the bondservants of our God on their** foreheads" **(Revelation 7:3).** We are in a time when the "four great winds of the earth" are in relative abeyance. There will be relative peace until the Lord has sealed His bondservants. *This is how we keep from receiving "the mark of the beast," by being sealed as a bondservant of God.* Satan cannot put his seal over God's seal.

How are we sealed as a bondservant? First we must understand that not all believers are bondservants. Many who claim the redemption of the blood of Christ go on living their lives for themselves. A bondservant is a slave of Christ. A slave has nothing of his own, including time, money, resources, even his family. We become bondservants when we have given everything to Him and hold nothing back.

We were bought with a price and we are not our own. The only way not to take the mark of the beast and become the devil's is to be the Lord's. Not a single one can be plucked from the Lord's hand. Money has always possessed the power to reveal who we really worship. It is fitting that the beast is an Economic power; at the end of the age Economics will be a major factor determining who we really belong to. How we handle our money and the assets entrusted to our stewardship is becoming more important every day.

An idol was not just something that the heathen worshipped, but it represented what they trusted in. Money has a way of revealing who we actually put our trust in, and who we are really serving—the world, the devil, ourselves, or the Lord. We must use the coming time of relative peace to get our houses in order in every way, but foremost we must learn to put our faith in God alone, in every area of our lives. There will be a time on this earth when true Christians will not be allowed to buy, sell or trade—now is the time for us to come to know the Lord as our Source of provision. As the psalmist wisely exhorted:

> **Therefore, let everyone who is godly pray to Thee in a time when Thou mayest be found; surely in a flood of great waters they shall not reach him (Psalm 32:6).**

The solution is not for all Christians to isolate themselves from the world and try to build self-sufficient communities. In the time to come we will not be able to trust in *ourselves* either. *Self*-sufficiency can be just as much an idol as any other source that we depend on. We must know the Lord as our Source and keep our trust in Him. He may direct some to build internally sufficient communities, but if we fall to putting our trust in the community we will still fall. *The key to our survival in this time is being a bond-slave. Every master is obligated to provide for his slaves, and we have the most dependable Master of all. He will take care of His own.*

Being a bond-servant of the Lord is to become His slave, but it also brings the greatest freedom we can ever know in this life. We are called to be dead to this world; when we are truly dead to the world there is nothing the world can do to us. It is impossible for a dead man to fear, to be offended, or to feel remorse because he loses some of his possessions. If we allow the fear of losing our possessions, or positions to control us, that is an indication they are still idols in our hearts. We are called to be dead to this world but alive to Christ. When we have Him all of the treasures of this earth seem petty and insignificant.

When Christ is our Life, our Trust, and the true desire of our heart, He can then trust us with earthly possessions and positions. But if He is not our Life, our Trust and the desire of our heart, our possessions and positions will inevitably rule over us. Whoever or whatever rules over us is in fact our lord. We are entering a time when the Lordship of Jesus must be more than a doctrine—it must be a profound and continuing reality in our life.

The Call

The kingdom of God is not built upon Military, Religious, Political or Economic foundations—it is built upon the Lordship of Jesus and His love, joy, peace, patience, kindness, goodness, faithfulness, gentleness, self-control. **"For the kingdom of God is not eating and drinking, but righteousness and peace and joy in the Holy Spirit" (Romans 14:17).** The kingdom of God transcends the earthly realms of power; the Lord Himself made clear: **"My kingdom is not of this world. If My kingdom were of this world, then My servants would be fighting,… but as it is, My kingdom is not of this realm"** (John 18:36).

If we are going to preach the kingdom of God, as His ambassadors representing His interests, if we are to exert its influence over the kingdoms of this earth, we must understand the difference between these realms of power. During each of the great transitional phases of the earthly power bases, the church has been severely tested and shaken in relation to her own power base. In each case much of the church went the way of the world and lost her spiritual relevance. In each case there were some who stood against the evil influence over the "winds of the earth" in such a way that they were then able to help direct them.

During the time of the shift from Military to Religious power bases, the greatest overall test of the hearts of men was in relation to their religious faith. During the next shift to the Political power base, it seemed that the energies of both heaven and hell were focused on redefining human governments and this also became a great test of human character. As we are now basically in the time of the Economic dominance of human affairs, finding the heart of God in dealing with Economic issues is crucial to our lives, our faith and our ministries.

In a sense, the forces of evil have been able to put their "mark" on men through the Military, Political or even the Religious power bases when men chose the way of evil over the way of the Lord. Even so, there is something particularly climactic and ultimate about the way that the "beast" uses the Economic power base in the last days. How the church continues to relate to all of the power bases is important, but how we relate to the world

Economy must now be a priority. Let us not waste the time that the Lord gives us by just trying to hold back the winds of the earth; instead we must give ourselves to serving the winds of heaven. There is a kingdom that cannot be shaken—let us build our lives entirely upon it—the time is coming when every thing else will be shaken. It is important that we not just know what the signs of the times are, but that we understand them and are prepared to take the action demanded by our Lord's own mandate to us.

Christian Economics

Christian economics will and should become a popular emphasis in the church. This is simply the emphasis of good stewardship. We have usually interpreted the Lord's parable of the talents in terms of how we should properly use either our natural talents or spiritual gifts (see Matthew 25:14-30). We should certainly seek to use everything that the Lord has entrusted to us in the most profitable way. We must understand that our spiritual gifts are more important than our natural resources. However, what is often overlooked is that in this parable the talents that the Lord referred to were money. In biblical times "talents" were a form of currency. Certainly we must not exclude the literal interpretation of this parable as well. Luke 16:9-13 records another important exhortation from the Lord:

And I say to you, make friends for yourselves by means of the mammon of unrighteousness;

that when it fails, they may receive you into the eternal dwellings.

He who is faithful in a very little thing is faithful also in much; and he who is unrighteous in a very little thing is unrighteous also in much.

If therefore you have not been faithful in the use of unrighteous mammon, who will entrust the true riches to you?

And if you have not been faithful in the use of that which is another's, who will give you that which is your own?

No servant can serve two masters; for either he will hate the one, and love the other, or else he will hold to one, and despise the other. You cannot serve God and mammon.

That we cannot serve God and mammon obviously means that we cannot combine the motive of serving God with the motive of making money. There is abundant evidence in both ancient and contemporary history that the love of money can quickly corrupt ministries. But we must not exclude the first part of the Lord's exhortation in this text, that we need to "make friends with unrighteous mammon." In this He is not telling us to be friends with the mammon, but to use mammon to make friends with.

We must learn to be faithful with worldly goods before we can be entrusted with the true riches of the kingdom. Learning to properly handle unrighteous mammon while maintaining a right spirit is important for every Christian. Learning to do this now, as the ultimate conflict between the spirit of this world and the kingdom of God begins to revolve around economics and the ability to "buy, sell and trade," makes this exhortation even more critical and timely.

Special Note

Space in this book does not allow for practical teachings on biblical economics, but this subject is addressed in depth in my book *Leadership, Management and the Five Essentials for Success*, which is also available through MorningStar Publications.

Chapter Three

The Powers Of The Age To Come

> For in the case of those who have once been enlightened and have tasted of the heavenly gift and have been made partakers of the Holy Spirit,
>
> *and have tasted the good word of God and the powers of the age to come,*
>
> and then have fallen away, it is impossible to renew them again to repentance, since they again crucify to themselves the Son of God, and put Him to open shame (Hebrews 6:4-6).

This text has been an enigma to many believers. The key phrase here is *"and* **have tasted the good word of God,** *and* **the powers of the age to come."** What is the "good word of God," and "the powers of the age to come?" Both of these will soon be released in the church. It is now crucial that we understand both the powers and their dangers.

The "good word of God" is the message of the kingdom. John the Baptist and the Lord Jesus preached this message. However, just as many of the most important doctrines of the faith were obscured after the first century A.D., the true gospel of the kingdom is yet to be recovered and preached by the last day church. This message is also represented in Revelation 11:15 as "the seventh trumpet." These trumpets are messages, and the seventh is the last message to be preached, which is: **"The kingdom of the world has become the kingdom of our Lord, and of His Christ; and He will reign forever and ever."**

The last day gospel will not just be one of salvation, but that Jesus reigns as King over all. He is seated above every authority and power. This message will come with the power that testifies of His place of ultimate authority. Unprecedented power will be released through the church when the time of this message has come.

The True Message Is Power

The true gospel was always meant to be preached with a power that demonstrated the authority of the word of God. It was for this reason that the apostle Paul declared that: **"... my message and my preaching were not in persuasive words of wisdom, but in demonstration of the Spirit and of power, that your faith should not rest on the wisdom of men, but on the power of God... For the kingdom of God does not consist in words, but in power" (I Corinthians 2:4-5, 4:20).** When the last day message goes forth in power, for a period of time it will seem like all of the miracles that accompanied Moses, Elijah and Paul will be combined with the preaching anointing of John the Baptist.

There will be many of these messengers of power, but this authority will only be entrusted to the most faithful and humble servants. For all of the glory that will be demonstrated, there is a corresponding danger. This "power of the age to come" involves much more than the gifts of healing and miracles commonly demonstrated in the church today. To whom much is given much is required, and those who are trusted with this power cross a line in the Spirit from which backsliding is not just grievous—it is catastrophic. To fall from such a place in the Spirit would represent the kind of utter corruption that was found in Satan, who dwelt in the very throne room of God, was "the cherub that covered," witnessing all of the glory of God, and still he transgressed.

For such a one who has seen this level of glory and still falls, it is "impossible to renew them again." One who has seen the highest realm of power and glory, without experiencing a profound change of heart, is corrupted beyond help. We may wonder, "Why then would the Lord allow such a one to experience this level of anointing?" It is for the same reason that he called Judas and included him in the innermost circle. The Lord knew from the beginning that Judas would betray him. He knew that he was a thief, yet He trusted him with the common purse. This was not to condemn Judas further, but to go as far as He could in giving him the opportunity to repent.

The blood of Jesus is enough to erase any sin, but we must embrace His grace to receive it. When a person crosses the line from which it is impossible to renew him, it is not because the power of the blood is lacking, but the will of that person is corrupted to the degree that he will not embrace the grace to be changed again. The nature of Judas will be found in some who even walk in the highest levels of authority in the last days. Their falls will bring great testing upon the church. Therefore we must always be careful not to judge men by their power, but by their fruit.

The Standard Of Divine Judgment

In Matthew 11:21-24, the Lord warned of a standard of divine judgment that many fail to comprehend. He said that it would actually be more tolerable for Sodom than for the cities of Judea who had rejected Him. By all outward appearances those cities of Judea were probably more righteous than any cities that have since existed on the face of the earth. They did not have abortions, pornography, or even the smallest degree of the kind of corruption that is almost universal in the west today. A person caught in adultery was stoned to remove even the trace of evil from their midst. Yet, Jesus said that one of the most wicked cities that ever existed would have it easier in the judgment than they would. How could this be?

The reason that Sodom will have it better than these "righteous" cities is that the Lord does not judge by the degree of darkness as much as by the degree of light that has been rejected. Sodom only had the witness of Lot; Chorazin and Bethsaida had the witness of the Son of God. There is grave responsibility that comes with every bit of light that we receive. Those who taste of the powers of the age to come are accountable for that great knowledge with which they have been trusted.

Does this mean that it would just be better not to seek the great light and power that is coming. Of course not! Then we will already have condemned ourselves as the Lord also warned: **"The Queen of the South shall rise up with the men of this generation at the judgment and condemn them, because she came from the ends of the earth to hear the wisdom of Solomon; and behold, something greater than Solomon is here"** (Luke 11:31). In other words, if the Queen of Sheba would travel so far just to hear Solomon, what a terrible disregard of the glory will we be guilty of for not pursuing what is available to us through Christ!

If we turn our backs on what the Lord is making available to us today we will end up gnashing our teeth in outer darkness. Those who end up that way are virgins who are waiting on the Bridegroom, but who are too foolish to fill their vessels with oil. The only choice that we have is to pursue the Lord with all of our hearts. As the truth and power of the age to come is demonstrated, whether through us or not, we will be held accountable for that light. This is only a warning that the frivolous kind of backsliding that many of us tolerate in our lives from time to time will become increasingly dangerous as the Lord begins to move in power.

It is dangerous for us to backslide to any degree at any time, as the Lord warned: **"The men of Nineveh shall stand up with this generation at the judgment and condemn it, because they repented at the preaching of Jonah; and behold, something greater than Jonah is here"** (Luke 11:32). We must not be discouraged from seeking to walk in the highest level of anointing and power, but we must also be sober about it, understanding the responsibility that comes with it.

Walking On Water

Water often represents mass humanity in Scripture. Isaiah 17:13 states: **"The nations rumble on like the rumbling of many waters, but He will rebuke them and they will flee far away...."** When the Lord rebuked the storm and the waves calmed down it was a prophetic fulfillment of this passage. It was also a prophetic statement that one day He would arise to rebuke the storms of this world, and the rising waves of humanity, and they would be stilled.

When the church is tossed about in her little boats, battered by the storms, then the Lord will come to her in the darkness of this great night, walking upon the waters. This understandably frightened the disciples more than the storm. However, Peter's response was remarkable. He requested that if this was indeed the Lord for Jesus to ask him to get out of the boat and walk on the waters with Him. All Jesus said was "Come," and Peter did, for a time walking upon the tossing waves with Jesus.

At the end of this age many Christians will duplicate Peter's exploit and walk on water. However, we must understand that Peter did not walk on the water; he walked on the command of the Lord. He was wise not to get out of the boat until he heard the Lord say, "come." When we walk in obedience to the command of God we do not need anything else under our feet. The word of God is much more solid than the earth or anything in it. This will be the message of those who demonstrate these astonishing miracles.

All of the great miracles and exploits of the church in the last hour will be the result of intimacy with the Lord, and utter obedience to the Holy Spirit. Until the end we will also have foolish, and misguided believers who will try to accomplish such feats as proof of their spirituality, which will result in humiliation and injury. Whenever we try to do something to prove ourselves we have departed from the true substance of faith that produces miracles. This was how the enemy tempted Jesus, to use miracles to prove who He was, and it is in this way that he continues to cause many of His followers to stumble. Miracles are given to testify of Jesus and the power of His kingdom, not to testify to who we are.

Counterfeits

There will also be many counterfeit miracles from the enemy in the last days. There are already cults that practice walking on hot coals or sharp knives. Many missionaries have witnessed the power of some witch doctors to fly from place to place through demonic power. These are all counterfeits of heavenly powers that have been demonstrated in the church, such as Philip being translated in Acts 8:39-40.

There will be witches and warlocks who will be able to duplicate even the great miracle of walking on water and air, but we must not let this discourage us from the importance of the real. The only proper response to the many counterfeit miracles is to pursue those which are true. Both the kingdom of God and the kingdom of darkness are established by power. In this last great battle of the kingdoms, those who abandon the true power of God will find themselves becoming increasingly subject to the counterfeit powers.

It was important for Moses to demonstrate all of the miracles that were given to him even though the Lord knew that some would be matched by the cultists of Egypt. These conflicts and power challenges are important for the maturity of the church. We must not let any kind of satanic duplication of what the Lord is doing discourage us. There will be a point at which the church goes far beyond any power manifested by the enemy. Then even the cultist will acknowledge the true power of God as being much greater than their power.

Our only defense against the counterfeit power of Satan is to know the true power of God. The power of God is easily distinguished from the powers of darkness because the power of the Holy Spirit will always glorify the Son of God. The power of darkness will always try to focus men's attention on those who demonstrate the power, leading to the glorification and worship of men.

Increased Temptations

As we grow in spiritual authority and walk in greater supernatural power, temptations will also increase. The enemy will especially use the tendency for men to covet some honor and glory for themselves to seduce the saints. Satan will try to get the church to give more attention to the manifestation of the sons of God than to the manifestation of the Son. Many will fall from grace, proclaiming that they are the ones that the whole creation has been waiting to behold. Those who succumb to declaring a gospel of the sons of God will be disqualified from attaining the very thing they are seeking. Those who walk in the high callings of God do so not for what they are seeking for themselves, but because they have abandoned themselves for the glory of the Son of God.

It is crucial for those who would walk in the power of the age to come to be delivered from the temptation to draw attention to themselves, their ministries, or even the church. Seeing Jesus receive the glory that is due Him must be our consuming and only passion. The more power that is released the more tempting it will be to use it for self-glorification. This is the very thing that caused Satan's fall and its power can seduce even the elect. We must now war against self-seeking and self-promotion like the deadly enemies that they are.

Every bit of influence that we gain through self-promotion will ultimately be a stumbling block to us, keeping us from the will of God. Every nickel that we raise through manipulation and self-promotion will be a stumbling block that can prevent us from fulfilling our calling and destiny. Our noble intentions for using such influence or resources are completely irrelevant; using such devices in an effort to accomplish the work of the Lord will disqualify us from being a significant part of the greater work that is coming. The Lord is now giving His church time to repent of human efforts and to learn to build upon the only foundation that will last—the Lord Jesus Himself and simple obedience to Him. It is spoken in Isaiah:

> **Sinners in Zion are terrified; Trembling has seized the godless. Who among us can live with the consuming fire? Who among us can live with continual burning?**
>
> **He who walks righteously, and speaks with sincerity, He who rejects unjust gain, and shakes his hands so that they hold no bribe..."** **(Isaiah 33:14-15).**

The Lord will be drawing increasingly close to His people as the end of this age draws near. The author of Hebrews declared: **"Our God is a consuming fire" (Hebrews 12:29)**, and His presence will consume the wood, hay and stubble. When we try to build on hype, manipulation and soul power what we build will be consumed. No one who takes bribes will be able to stand in His presence, but how easily do we still take them! How easily we will determine the meetings that we should take by the amount of the honorarium or offerings, which is nothing less than taking a bribe. How easily we allow the most generous givers to dictate policy in our churches and ministries, which is nothing less than taking a bribe. As long as we do this we are only storing up greater pain for that wonderful time when He comes closer, because we will not be able to abide in His presence. Isaiah continues:

> **But there the majestic One, the Lord, shall be for us a place of rivers and wide canals, on which no boat with oars shall go, and on which no mighty ship shall pass (Isaiah 33:21).**

"Boats with oars" speak of vessels propelled by human energy. Such will not be allowed on the way that the Lord is preparing. Paul explained to the men of Athens, "human hands cannot serve Him," and that which is propelled by human strength cannot accomplish the purposes of God. That no "mighty ships" will be allowed speaks of huge, cumbersome ministries. Not only are these unable to maneuver in the streams of God, but they block the paths of those who can.

Walking On Air

The Lord Jesus said: **Truly, truly I say to you, he who believes in Me, the works that I do, shall he do also; and greater works than these shall he do; because I go to the Father (John 14:12).** In a dream the Lord showed me what one of these greater works would be—walking on air! I saw a man of God who was ministering to a great crowd of people. He wanted to lay hands on a sick woman near the back of the crowd, but there was no way for him to get to her because of the press of the people. He hesitated briefly and then walked on the air above the crowd until he reached her. The people were so astonished that many of them fell on their backs as a great roar of praise to God arose from them.

The man of God seemed embarrassed but resolute as he came to the woman and laid hands on her to be healed. In the dream the man's demeanor was just as amazing as his miracle of walking on the air above the people. This was obviously not done for show, but because it had to be done to accomplish the purpose of God in ministering to this woman. I was also given the understanding that this man had walked on air many times before, in private, out of necessity, and he very reluctantly had revealed his authority to do this to the people. This will not be a frivolous trick for the purpose of impressing people, but a witness to one of the most profound truths of the gospel of the kingdom—*that the word of God is of greater substance than terra firma.*

Those who know how to keep secrets, who have the discretion to maintain silence until the proper time, will be trusted with the authority to do the greatest exploits. Many cannot keep such things a secret out of a genuine desire to testify of the Lord and His grace, but this is nevertheless a flaw that renders them unworthy for the greater authority. **"The *secret* of the Lord is for those who fear Him" (Psalm 25:14).**

Just as the Lord did some of His greatest miracles in private, or only in the presence of His closest disciples, the Lord wants to do many of His great works in relative obscurity. This may seem incomprehensible, but our lack of comprehension only reveals a human perspective, just as it did when the Lord's own brothers said to Him:

"Depart from here, and go into Judea, that Your disciples also may behold Your works which You are doing. For no one does anything in secret, when he himself seeks to be known publicly..." (John 7:3-4).

The key phrase here is *"For no one does anything in secret when he himself seeks to be known publicly."* Jesus was not doing things to become known, but He "emptied Himself" and became of "no reputation" in order to fulfill His calling. He became as humble as He could, being born in a stable, raised in Nazareth as a peasant, and finally suffering the most humiliating death ever devised by demented men. His entire devotion was to embrace humility so that He could glorify the Father.

In contrast, there is a mentality present in ministry that we cannot accomplish the purpose of God without making ourselves known. So we try to get as much visibility for our ministries as possible. These are the Lord's children, and they honestly do often have good intentions, even if they are mixed, so He will use them as much as He can. However, just as good is often the worst enemy of best; such a mentality will disqualify us from the highest purposes of the kingdom.

John the Baptist did not have to dress for power. He did not have to go up to Jerusalem—all of Jerusalem would come out to him. Why did they come? Because of his slick advertising? Because of his eloquence? Because he had an excellent choir? No. They came because he was anointed. The only thing that would attract anyone to John was the anointing. The only thing that would attract anyone to Jesus was the anointing. They had no props, no devices, no advertising agency. All they had was the Holy Spirit, but He was all they needed. Until we come to the place that the Holy Spirit is all that we need for our ministry, we will not receive all that the Holy Spirit has.

This is the wisdom of the high calling. **"He who speaks from himself seeks his own glory [literally "recognition"]; but He who is seeking the glory of the One who sent Him, He is true, and there is no unrighteousness in Him" (John 7:18).** The degree to which self-seeking enters our ministry is the degree to which it has been corrupted. Conversely, to the degree that we seek the glory of the Son of God, that is the degree to which He will be able to trust us with the authority of the kingdom.

The authority of the kingdom is the ability to bring the influence of the kingdom into this earthly realm. How much we have built our ministries on influence from the earthly realm will determine the degree to which we have disqualified ourselves from true kingdom authority. The degree to which we have built our lives on the power, witness, and fruit of the Holy Spirit will determine the degree to which He can use us in this awesome time to come.

Chapter Four

Restoring The Pastor Ministry

"And He gave some as apostles, and some as prophets, and some as evangelists, and some as pastors and teachers,

for the equipping of the saints for the work of service, to the building up of the body of Christ;

until we all attain to the unity of the faith, and of the knowledge of the Son of God, to a mature man, to the measure of the stature which belongs to the fullness of Christ (Ephesians 4:11-12).

A portion of the body of Christ has devoted itself to "equipping the saints for the work of service," and with some measure of success. As the passage above continues, this is essential if the church is going to mature to the stature to which we have been called, being nothing less than the stature of the fullness of Christ. Even though this has been one of the most evaluated, discussed, and taught passages over the last several decades within the advancing church, it is about to receive an even greater impetus.

The church is about to go through a needed time of re-evaluating its definitions of these "equipping ministries." The result is going to be a much greater clarity of function for each of them, and a much greater flow of true ministry throughout the whole church. The ministry that may experience the most profound changes in this process will be that of the pastor. The result of these changes will not bring less significance in its place of ministry in the church, but one that is pivotal for releasing the other ministries and gifts into their fullness.

What Is A Pastor?

Ephesians 4:11 quoted above is the only place in the New Testament where the word "pastor" is found. Neither is there a description of the duties of this ministry given anywhere in the New Testament. Yet, today almost the entire ministry of the church revolves around this one office. How did a ministry that is but once mentioned, and is not even once described, come to so dominate the life of the body of Christ? Is this the way the Lord designed the ministry of His church?

We must understand that the amount of attention given a certain subject in Scripture does not necessarily reflect its level of importance. Most evangelicals would consider the need to be "born again" one of the most essential doctrines in Christianity, yet it is only briefly mentioned twice in Scripture, with no real definition of its meaning given. When the Lord gives something with such importance so little definition, it compels us to seek Him for both the understanding and the experience. It is more important to be born again than to be able to describe it. In fact, being born again is impossible to understand until it is experienced.

It is apparent that the Lord was ambiguous about the role of the pastor ministry in the church precisely because of its great importance, not the lack of it. The pastor ministry is actually much more, not less, than the present, popular model. However, it is radically different in many ways.

The present popular model of the pastor ministry has usurped much of the responsibility delegated to the other equipping ministries listed in Ephesians 4:11. It has also had much of its responsibility usurped, mostly by the spirit of the world, or "secular humanism." Finding the Lord's definition for this ministry is imperative if the church is going to come into the authority and power required to accomplish her mandate for these times, which is to overcome this spirit of the world.

All of the ministries are the manifestation of an aspect of the Lord's own ministry. Jesus was the Apostle, the Prophet, the Evangelist, the Shepherd and the Teacher. Serving in any ministry is simply becoming a vessel through whom the Lord can reveal Himself to touch the needs of His people. A man is not a teacher just because he is articulate, or has accurate doctrine, but because the Teacher lives in him. Likewise, a pastor is not just someone with a degree or ordination papers from a certain institution or organization, but a man through whom The Shepherd has chosen to reveal that aspect of His ministry. The most accurate example of a true Pastor is found in observing the Lord's own ministry as the Great Shepherd.

One For All And All For One

Many try to recognize modern prophetic ministries by relating them to their Old Covenant counterparts, but this is a mistake. The Old Covenant prophet usually stood alone, while the New Covenant prophet is but one part of the equipping ministry of the church, and must function in proper harmony with the others to fulfill his calling. The same is true with the pastor. Modern trends have often caused pastors to try to stand alone in ministry, but this ministry will never come into its proper place of authority and release until it works in harmony with the other ministries given to the church.

Many have tried to define the pastor by including the Lord's entire ministry—the apostolic, prophetic, evangelistic and teaching aspects, resulting in a tragic over-burdening and distortion of the true ministry. This is probably the main reason why many modern pastors try to be all things to their people, which greatly dilutes their effectiveness in the sphere of authority to which they have been called.

Failing to understand the God-ordained separation of responsibilities in ministry is a major cause of the devastating overload to the average pastor. For this reason many insurance companies now consider pastors "high risk." One insurance agent told me that many 35 year-old pastors have 65 year-old hearts. This is a major cause for the burnout many pastors now suffer after just a few years of service. Just as tragically, a major portion of the Lord's ministry to His church is not fulfilled, resulting in her not being properly equipped for the work of the ministry, not to mention the grievous weakness of the entire body.

No ministry can function properly unless it is properly related to the other ministries given to the church. None of the New Testament ministries are complete within themselves. All will be out of balance, and out of the will of the Lord, to the degree that they are not in harmony with the other ministries.

The present emphasis on the restoration of the prophetic ministry to the church should also result in a *further* restoration of the other equipping ministries. Each ministry is required for the full definition of the others. None will come into their full spiritual authority and anointing until they are all properly restored and related to their appointed place and stature.

Even though the modern pastor ministry may have often assumed authority or responsibilities that were not given to it, much of this has been done out of necessity because the other ministries were not functioning properly. As the other ministries assume their correct responsibilities, and each can become more specialized, each will realize a great increase in true spiritual authority. Like a laser, as we are each able to focus, more power will be released.

Many have seen their spiritual authority eroded because they assumed authority in realms where they had not been given it. When we stay within the realm that the Lord has appointed to us we are yoked with Him. When we are properly yoked with Him we have His authority, and this makes the yoke easy to carry. When we take yokes that the Lord has not given to us they are always heavy, sapping us of our strength and our anointing. The Lord is now working to bring about a great repositioning in his church, one that will bring us all into our proper place, which will result in a significant increase in our anointing and effectiveness.

As we come into the harvest that is the end of this age, it is imperative that we are in our assigned sphere of authority or we will be overwhelmed with what is coming upon us. Even though the typical, modern pastoral ministry may be carrying many responsibilities and burdens which it has not been called to carry, it is called to have far *more* responsibility than it now has. The only way that those with this ministry will ever fulfill their calling is by having every yoke but the Lord's yoke removed from them.

The King's Master Chef

The Greek word translated "pastor" in Ephesians 4:11 could be literally translated *"a feeder."* This reveals the basic function of this ministry—to feed the Lord's sheep. We may think that this is really the function of the teaching ministry which is listed after the pastor, but that is a different Greek word, which could be more accurately translated "instructor."

Because of the seeming overlap of the pastor and teaching ministries, and with it being difficult to distinguish "feeding" the Lord's sheep from "instructing" them, many have concluded that Paul was really addressing one ministry—the pastor/teacher rather than the pastor ministry *and* the teacher ministry. In many cases there is a combination of these gifts in a single person. However, there are also many gifted teachers who have little pastoring ability, and there are many gifted pastors who are not gifted as teachers.

The difference between "feeding" and "instructing" is that feeding has to do with providing the spiritual diet, while instructing has more to do with developing skills in a person. At a university the chef would do the feeding, but the professors would do the instructing. As a flight instructor I did not just impart knowledge about aircraft; I got into the airplane with the student to help them develop their skills as a pilot.

Perhaps our pastor does all of this for us, but herein lies the question: Is he supposed to do all of this? Would he not have much higher quality spiritual food to serve if he was not trying to do the instructing as well, but rather relied on others to help believers apply their knowledge?

The feeding of the Lord's sheep is critical; it must be given the very highest priority. We do not want to give the King's own household "junk food!" In biblical times, as we can see in Joseph's story, the baker (chef) was one of the king's most trusted and honored servants. What chef, who was given the commission to prepare meals for the president, or any potentate, would not put his very best into each meal? Such a chef would probably scour the world for the best ingredients for every dish, hire only the best assistants, and seek out only the best dinnerware on which to serve it. How much more should we put our best into what we serve the Lord's own household, whom we have been given this great honor of serving?

Who Then Is In Charge?

In the Lord's discourse concerning the end times, He includes a challenging statement that is obviously directed at the pastor ministry:

> **Who then is the faithful and sensible slave whom his master put in charge of his household to give them their food at the proper time?**
>
> **Blessed is that slave whom his master finds so doing when he comes (Matthew 24:45-46).**

To the consternation of the idealists who consider the present authority of the typical modern pastor as excessive, here we see that the ones whom the Lord calls to feed His sheep are "put in charge of his household." Because of the importance of His people having the proper spiritual food, the Lord has made the "chef" the manager of His entire house. Even so, this does not mean that he must personally do everything.

We also see from the text in Matthew 24 that *timing* is crucial. There are certain foods that are appropriate to certain times of the year, and even certain times of the day. The Lord expects His pastors to be sensitive to the times, and the *present* needs of those whom he has been entrusted to serve. The "sensible slave" was the one who gave His household their food "at the proper time." This in itself is a full time job.

Loving The Lord And Tending The Sheep

In a literal translation of John chapter 21, the Lord asked Peter if he loved Him. After Peter's affirmative response the Lord then directed Peter to "feed My lambs." Then the Lord asked Peter again, and after the affirmative response He exhorted him to "tend My sheep." After the third time, He directed Peter to "feed My sheep." Here the Lord is actually giving three different instructions to Peter. First to *feed* the *lambs*, then to *tend* the *sheep*, then to *feed* the *sheep*.

The Lord made a distinction between "feeding" and "tending," and most shepherds would agree that there is a distinction. To feed the sheep is to lead them to a proper pasture. To tend them would include protecting them from predators and parasites, nursing them when they become sick, breaking up fights, etc., which are all typical of the modern pastor's duties. The Lord also distinguished between the lambs and the sheep, obviously concerned that neither group be forgotten.

It is also important that the lambs were to be fed before the sheep. If the lambs are not taken care of first they are often overlooked. Even so, the charge is to feed both. This has proven to be a difficult balance for many congregations to find. Either they will gravitate toward emphasizing food for the younger believers, or for those who are more mature. To have a healthy flock, neither can be overlooked.

In this passage we should also consider that the children are literal and not just spiritual. Many churches try to find ways to baby sit the children so that they can minister to the adults. In this we may have our priorities backwards. The Lord would have us to consider the care of children before the adults, lest they are forgotten or are just given the leftovers. If we put our highest priority on the children, by the time they became adults many of them would be shepherds themselves rather than requiring so much of our continued attention and ministry.

It is also noteworthy that the Lord based Peter's responsibility to the sheep on his love for Him, not for the sheep. Of course Peter was to love the sheep, but the foundation of this ministry was a love for the Lord, not the people. The first commandment is to love the Lord, and then each other. If we get this backwards it will not be true, godly, love that is the foundation of our ministry. If we love the Lord more than we love His people, we will love His people more than we would otherwise. If we love the people, or the ministry, more than we love the Lord, we have become idolaters and will become unrighteously possessive, ultimately becoming barriers between the Lord and His people. The more that we love the Lord, the more that we will be prone to *properly* care for His people.

The Domain Of The Mind

It is in this area of "tending" the sheep where much of a true pastor's authority and responsibility has been usurped by philosophies based on secular humanism. One of the fundamental needs of a Christian once he has been born again is to have his mind renewed, of which Paul exhorts in Romans:

I urge you therefore, brethren, by the mercies of God, to present your bodies a living and holy sacrifice, acceptable to God, which is your spiritual service of worship.

And do not be conformed to this world, but be transformed by the renewing of your mind, that you may prove what the will of God is, that which is good and acceptable and perfect (Romans 12:1-2).

According to this Scripture, our minds must be renewed before we can prove what the will of God is. For a Christian to "walk in the light" he must live by a different perspective, knowledge and understanding than is prevalent in the world. Yet, the domain of knowledge and understanding has almost universally been given over to the world in everything from education to mental health. Both education and "mental health" are the very essential, basic domains of the pastor ministry in the church. These must be recovered if the pastor ministry is going to be restored to its proper place in the church.

Many Christians still think and perceive from the world's perspective because the world is essentially in control of the development of their minds. This is in fundamental conflict with the Spirit. As we read in Ephesians:

If indeed you have heard Him and have been taught in Him, just as truth is in Jesus,

that, in reference to your former manner of life, you lay aside the old self, which is being corrupted in accordance with the lusts of deceit,

and that you *be renewed in the spirit of your mind,*

and put on the new self, which in the likeness of God has been created in righteousness and holiness of the truth (Ephesians 4:21-24).

The world's educational systems and mental health philosophies are in basic conflict with the renewing process that would remake us into the likeness of Christ. In fact, almost everything about these philosophies promote the development and dominance of what the Scripture refers to as "the old man," the "carnal nature," or the "flesh." Can we turn our children over to the world's schools, which are founded on the religion of secular humanism, to have their minds formed and then expect them to be Christlike and spiritually discerning?

PART II

The Pastoral Mandate For Education

Until the turn of this century, schools were generally the domain of the church. Most of the great universities were founded by the church, but we have abdicated our responsibility in the field of education and turned it over to the world. To educate means to enlighten. The church was called to be "the light of the world," which means basically we are called to educate the world according to the ways of God. The church has a mandate in the area of education that must be recovered. There are political and legal considerations to this, but can there be any barrier to the will of God?

Do I believe in Christian schools? Absolutely! In fact, if anything, I do not believe in public schools, which are a fundamental reflection of the failure of the church. I say this with the fullest respect for the *proper* separation between church and state. However, "public schools" are fundamentally religious in nature, promoting the religion of secular humanism, regardless of their claims.

Understanding the creation is *fundamental* to religion. If there is a God who made us then He has a right to our worship and to dictate our lifestyle. If we do not believe that we were created, but rather evolved from slime, then we will worship ourselves. That is essentially what secular humanism is—the idolatrous worship of man. Public schools that teach evolution are teaching the religion of secular humanism—the worship of man as his own god.

Reasons For Our Failure

Does this mean that we are sinning against our children by sending them to public schools? In a general sense, yes, but in an individual sense, possibly not. In a general sense the whole church has failed because we have abdicated a basic responsibility given to the church, and specifically the pastor ministry. As individuals, many do not have a choice but to send their children to public schools, and the Lord obviously has grace for them.

Some children are also sent to public schools by the Lord as genuine missionaries. They are salt and light. However, if we are sending our children to public school just because we cannot afford to send them to Christian school, I believe that we would be better to cut off any or all luxuries, or maybe even some needs, to send them to a Christian school. We simply cannot afford not to do this.

However, it is true that some parents could sacrifice even down to the barest necessities and not be able to afford to send their children to a Christian school. This is but another glaring failure of the church. Why are Christian schools not affordable, or even free, for the children of believers?

There are usually several reasons for this. One of the most common reasons relates to the church's priorities. If the church in general spent the resources on educating her children that is spent on unnecessary buildings, or the programs that they develop to draw people when they do not have the anointing to attract them, many churches could today have a school that would be the envy of the world.

Even so, the primary reason why Christian schools are unavailable for most Christian children, or are so expensive, is the lack of unity in the church. Not every congregation is called to have a school. Some congregations who have attempted to establish their own school have even been destroyed by it, and many others have suffered divisions or other serious wounds. However, if the church in just a typical school district would unite for the purpose of educating her children it could provide quality schools which would surpass that of any public or other private school. If the congregations who did not have the calling to establish a school would contribute their fair share to those who did, all would benefit through our ability to specialize on what we do best.

This subject cannot be adequately covered here, but because of the times and the impending exponential increase of evil, this is an issue that must now be addressed by the church. The longer we wait to address it the more difficult it will be for us all—especially the children. Presently the wheels are coming off of most public schools. Not only is the evil that is taught, and tolerated, in public schools increasing dramatically—many are now becoming war zones. This lack of authority and control is the result of their denial of the ultimate authority—God.

Evangelism Through Education

It is also important that we do not form Christian schools out of a "ghetto mentality" of trying to escape the world. We cannot be the light of the world if we are cut off from the world. This is why many Christian leaders are in opposition to forming Christian schools, but the mandate of God for this is actually the reverse. The Lord wants us to develop schools of such quality, order and peace that the heathen will beat a path to our doors to educate their children. This can become one of the church's greatest evangelistic tools, and possibly its greatest opportunity to impact the next generation for the sake of righteousness, sowing salt and light throughout the nation.

Many congregations, denominations, and movements have already taken much ground in this area, and we need to learn from them so that we do not each have to "re-invent the wheel." There are serious difficulties with most Christian schools, but they must be addressed and overcome through the Spirit who has given us this mandate. The ultimate answers to many of our problems cannot be found until the church comes into unity. The church cannot fully accomplish its mandate in any area without unity. As churches start working together in the area of education they will also begin to realize their common interests in other areas. Every "joint" that is formed by two parts of the body coming together will build up the whole church.

Home Schooling

Home schooling is an answer for many, and often provides a superior education to public and private schools. Not only can home schooling provide special bonding within families, but it allows for an even greater ability to focus on the special needs, and gifts, of individual children. The quality of education that is being realized through home schooling is now being recognized, and encouraged by some state governments, rather than just tolerated.

With the new, easy to use curriculums designed especially for home schoolers now available, and being constantly upgraded, the home schooling movement is becoming a major, and important force in the field of education. It is not for everyone, but for those who choose this route it is proving to be extremely beneficial in preparing the next generation for their life and calling in the world.

Many who are home schooling their children are also forming support groups to provide extracurricular activities, science, physical education facilities and for highly specialized types of instruction. This is giving birth to a type of education that seems to capture the best of home schooling and private schooling. This also provides the children with plenty of interaction with other children.

It is obvious that a great part of the confusion and disorientation that many teenagers suffer is the result of too much interaction with other children, which magnifies the effects of peer pressure. Until the twentieth century most children had far more interaction with adults than with other children. With the institution of public schools this changed drastically. Now for most children school is the central influence in their life, and they spend far more of their time with other children than with adults. This results in many having their basic values influenced more by other children than by their parents.

Regardless of how we educate our children, and certainly there are now a variety of valid options, we cannot keep giving our children over to the world to have their minds formed and then expect them to be godly! **"For the mind set on the flesh is death, but the mind set on the Spirit is life and peace" (Romans 8:6).**

If we are going to be the "light of the world," we must provide the world with its enlightenment. The church must address this if we are going to fulfill our mandate, and prove our love for the Lord by "tending" His sheep, properly. When the church does, in unity, properly address her mandate for education, the properly renewed minds of Christian children and youth will astonish and light up the world with their brilliance.

Pastor Or Principal?

If you are a pastor and have read this far, you may have started to come under a heavy burden. It is probably hard to fathom how it would be possible to take on any other responsibilities, much less one as expansive and great as establishing and overseeing a Christian school. Please relax! Most pastors are not called to do this, but if you are, this is the Lord's yoke and you will actually find rest and refreshment for your soul by doing it. However, before we can get His yoke on we must get rid of all of the ones that He did not put on us!

Most pastors are not called to be the principal or overseer of a Christian school, but for those who are, it may be their primary calling, not a stepping stone to "a real pastorate." Children are not second rate citizens in the kingdom, and children's pastors are not second rate pastors. In God's eyes these are some of the most important positions in the church. We must view children's and youth pastors as "real" pastors and give them the authority due this ministry. Pastoring children properly often requires helping the parents, which requires authority with adults as well if it is to be done properly.

It is true that the *primary* responsibility for the education of children lies with the parents, not the pastor. However, having the responsibility for educating our children does not necessarily mean that we do it all. Paul explained to the Corinthians that they had "many teachers, but not many fathers." For a proper education it is likely that my children will need to study subjects that I am not qualified to teach. It is not my place to teach those subjects, but it is my responsibility to see that they have the proper teacher for them. No one will replace me as my children's father, but many different teachers may be required to properly equip them for their lives and callings.

Neither can children's pastors, or Sunday school teachers, take my place as their father. I am the one who should provide the primary spiritual leadership for my children, but we all need the help of the ministries given to the church for this purpose.

One of the greatest onslaughts of the enemy in history is directed at trying to destroy the emerging generation. This onslaught comes because of their destiny. The churches of the future, or possibly *with* a future, are those who would rather entertain and "baby sit" the adults so that they can equip the children.

The present generation has not heeded its mandate to walk in its calling and possess its promised land, but the next one will. The Lord is now looking for the "Joshuas and Calebs" from the present generation who will lead those into their destiny. The spiritually discerning are not trying to make the children like them, but are trying to become more like the children so that they too can enter the kingdom. There is no building program, or program at all, that will pay the dividends like those which we invest in our children. If we really love the Lord we will properly care for both His sheep and His lambs.

True Church

Our children's spiritual education and equipping is more important than their vocational education. Their spiritual education must be the foundation for all other learning, and this cannot be accomplished in just a couple of hours on Sunday. The church is presently in bondage to its four walls and its four hours. True church is twenty-four hours a day, seven days a week—it is in session continually in every household and on every job.

The true gifts of the Spirit do not just function at eleven o'clock Sunday morning and seven o'clock on Wednesdays. We should be open to the spirit of prophecy at any time and anywhere. Neither do the true gifts have to come with all of the bombast *we* often attach to them, which is a stumbling block to unbelievers, as well as many believers. The Lord never meant for His church to be limited in the ways that it now is, and He never meant for education, which should fundamentally be the "renewing of our minds," to be limited to a classroom. *Life is meant to be our classroom.* In the Lord's school we never graduate, we just keep advancing.

True Academics

This is not to negate the proper place of academics, which often requires classroom facilities. The Christian, more than any other, should excel in academics. Everything that we do is supposed to be done "as unto the Lord," and academics should be viewed as a means to help prepare us for His service with even greater excellence.

True science is not in conflict with Christianity—true science will always lead to the Creator and reveal His Christ because **"all things have been created by Him and for Him… in Him all things hold together" (Colossians 1:16-17).** Jon Amos Comenius, who is called "the father of modern education," and was one of the greatest leaders of the historic Moravian Church, once stated, "Nature is God's second book." The apostle Paul said it this way, **"For since the creation of the world His invisible attributes, His eternal power and divine nature, have been clearly seen, being understood through what has been made..." (Romans 1:20).** Science should be a special domain of the true faith, and Christians, more than any others, should excel in it. True science includes seeking to behold the glory of God in creation as well as the proper use of creation.

The firm foundation that Comenius sought to establish through education was that Christ had triumphed, that Christ was The Truth, and therefore truth would always ultimately win over error. He believed that Jesus had overcome sin, and that His kingdom was continuing to move forward in history. He saw light as stronger than darkness, peace and justice stronger than violence, and the love of God, so prevalent in His creation that it would prevail in His new creation men.

The primary purpose of Christian education must never be to try to escape the world, but to shine His light into the world. We are not called to just show a better way, but The Way. Christ Jesus is revealed in everything that was made, and He is the Reason for everything that exists. In this way true worship and love for the Creator compels us to true education, and true science, as each should magnify the Lord in our hearts. In this there must be structure and discipline, but structure and discipline that is born out of the most sublime purpose—that of seeking Christ.

PART III

The Pastoral Mandate For Mental Health

Another foundational responsibility delegated to the pastor ministry is in the area that we now call "mental health." The authority entrusted to the church through this ministry has also come under a systematic attack through secular humanism. The amount of ground lost by the church through this assault has been a significant reason for the great increase in crime, violence and the overall disregard for life. However, there will be a full recovery of this mandate by the church, which will give the church spiritual authority over some of the most frightening evil powers now being released in the world.

First, the church must recover the biblical perspective of what mental health really is. The only true mental health that we can ever know is Christ-centricity. Christ is the Center of the universe, and everything that does not revolve around Him is eccentric (off center) and, to that degree, in delusion. To be "normal" according to the world's definition is to be in a state of serious mental imbalance. True mental health will only be attained when our minds have been renewed, when we have been delivered from the spirit of this world, and have taken on the mind of Christ.

The Basic Christian Faith

Fundamental to the church recovering her power and glory is the recovery of the basic truth that *the answer to all of our problems is found at the cross.* Through the cross we have been given the power to heal any disease—physical, spiritual or mental. If we are without the solution to a problem it is because we are not fully ministering in the power of the cross. When we are confronted with problems that are out of our ranges they are meant to drive us to the throne of grace to find God's grace and answers. God's throne of grace is the cross, through which we receive the power of God and the grace of God to overcome every human problem. *There is no problem found on earth that cannot be overcome through Christ.*

Inroads Of The New Age

For all of the attention that the church has given to the inroads of the New Age Movement into the church, we are soon going to wake up to the fact that an even more devastating infiltration has come through psychology, psychiatry and psychoanalysis than through all other sources combined. These have all worked to fundamentally turn men from the cross in their greatest area of need—the renewing of their minds. Pastors who turn God's people over to secular mental health professionals for help have made a fundamental departure from their calling, and have, in many cases, delivered the Lord's own sheep into the hands of wolves.

Does this mean that all psychologist and psychiatrists are wolves? No. Many of them are actually sheep in wolves clothing—they are well meaning people who have taken on the wrong garments. We should not spend our time attacking psychology or psychiatry; these methods were only developed in order to fill the vacuum produced because the church abdicated her authority in this area. They are trying desperately to help fallen men from the consequences of the fall because we will not do it. In many cases this is the very noble attempt of drowning men trying to help their fellow drowning men. Meanwhile, the church sits on the life preservers and pays no attention to the whole world that is drowning around her.

Psychological sciences have, in some ways, done an admirable job of illuminating the source of many "mental" problems. It is their remedy that must be challenged. Several studies have shown that people overcome "mental" problems faster with no help at all than with the help of a "professional." Many of those who were "helped," may feel better, but are even further from the truth and from the power of true deliverance than ever. Our goal is not to feel better about ourselves, but to be Christlike. This sometimes requires that we not feel better about ourselves, but that we allow "godly sorrow" to move us to genuine repentance. Only repentance will lead us to the cross where we find the only real answer for every human need.

Secular psychology at its best is humanistic, and it is often diabolical. An important question now being asked by many in the church is whether we should include "Christian psychology" or "inner healing" in this? I am not familiar enough with how these have become "Christian" to take a position on them. The Christian counselors that I have met were sincerely trying to help their fellow Christians, and some even acknowledged that they were only trying to fill the void abdicated by the church. I have recognized a true pastor's calling on some of these Christian counselors, and I could not help but wonder why there was no place for them in the church. How could a pastor call himself a pastor if he must send his people to outsiders for counseling? Counseling is basic to the pastor ministry, and if we cannot handle it we should change our title. This is not to infer that they should leave the ministry, or even the leadership of the church, but to call them a pastor is a misnomer.

Why Heal The Old Man?

Regardless of whether someone calls himself a Christian psychologist, counselor, or pastor, we must understand that any doctrine or practice that has as its prescription for our healing *the digging up of our "old man"* to get him healed, is making a grave mistake. We can blame our present condition on our potty training if we want to, and it may have honestly had something to do with it, but why not just bury it, go to the cross, and be transformed into a new man?

Even television news magazines have been blowing the whistle on the practice of some psychologists and inner healing specialists as dangerous, and often tragic.

It has been the practice of some, while seeking to locate the blame for their patient's problem, to plant in the "sub-conscious" memories of their patients, child abuse, molestation and other violations *which never took place*. Some of the psychologists interviewed actually justified this practice by saying that it helped their patients to feel better about themselves! No one seemed concerned about the families that were ruined, or the relationships between parents and their children that were forever destroyed. This will be the source of some of the enemy's most devastating attacks on families and churches in the days to come.

Many who claim to have been "helped" by psychology or inner healing may honestly feel better, but have been made chronically self-centered. From what were they helped? As Paul lamented, **"But I am afraid, lest as the serpent deceived Eve by his craftiness, your minds should be led astray from the simplicity and purity of devotion to Christ" (II Corinthians 11:3).** All of the psychology that is needed for this life is found in the Scriptures and we must learn to categorically reject that which has its source anywhere else.

Regardless of the abuses, the answer is not to attack psychology, but to return to the cross where the answers to every human problem are found. The Lord intends to do more than just show the world a few people who have overcome their depression or low self-esteem. He wants to reveal "new creation" men, women, children and families who have been delivered from all of the power of the enemy, and all of the consequences of the fall.

If we are going to fulfill the true shepherd ministry of Jesus in the church, we must first recover the fundamental Christian truth that Jesus is the answer to all of the world's problems, period. Everyone who is called to the pastor ministry has the power of that cross at his disposal, to give to everyone in need. Let us stop turning to any other prop or device that will never truly heal or deliver.

It is the truth that sets people free. If we do not have the truth that can deliver people from their bondage, we do not have the truth of the gospel. "Healing is the children's bread." Basic to feeding the Lord's sheep is healing them, mentally, physically and spiritually.

The pastor ministry involves far more than we have perceived, and through it the Lord is going to fully reveal His nature as the Good Shepherd who is the answer for every human need and problem. We do have a long way to go to recover all that this ministry is meant to be, but we must never be satisfied with anything less than a full recovery. Through this recovery all of the ministries given to the church will be able to take their proper place, and the glorious revealing of the Lord's own nature as the Good Shepherd will be fully revealed to the world again.

Basic to the recovery of the pastor ministry is the understanding that no one man can possibly fulfill the whole ministry of shepherd to the Lord's people, even in one congregation. Much of the responsibility of this ministry has been abdicated to secular professionals because we have often tried to force the entire ministry upon just one person who we call *the* pastor. If we are going to fulfill our own ministries we must start working in teams with the other equipping ministries given to the church, just as the Lord Himself did as an example.

The true maturity and authority of every pastor will be reflected in the maturity and authority of his team. Pastors are not called to be executives, or managers, but ministers of the grace and power of God. The true essence of this ministry must be recovered if the church is going to accomplish her mandate in this hour, but it will never happen until all human yokes placed upon it are removed.

Chapter Five

The Prophetic Power Of Music

Music is accurately called "the universal language." It is a communication media that can cross almost any geographical, ideological or racial barrier. Music has a unique ability to touch the soul and arrest the heart—it is a language of the spirit. Those who know this language and can use it effectively have been entrusted with a potent weapon in the battle for the hearts of men. Anointed music will be one of the church's biggest guns in the battle of the last days.

It is important that we comprehend just how powerful music is as a spiritual force. However, like "the force" in the Star Wars movies, it can be used for both good and evil. As witnessed during the 1960's and 70's, music can prophesy and sustain major sociological shifts like the erosion of moral foundations. It can also fuel revivals and spiritual awakenings such as the great Salvation Army movement, and the Welsh Revival at the turn of the century. The Lord is raising up a host of warriors who are now fighting to seize this music battleground from the enemy and use it for the kingdom. The Lord is about to anoint prophetic minstrels who will capture the world's attention, and communicate powerful truths through song that will help set the course for the last day ministry.

Artists and musicians usually foresee and foretell the social direction of civilization. Likewise, Christian artists and musicians often have the prophetic insight to be in touch with the trends and forces that are impacting the course of the world. Unfortunately, Christian artists with such insight are often constrained by the political and religious pressures in the church that can so inhibit creativity. Pioneers who are compelled by their vision often must break ranks with the religious status quo to explore new regions. This places them in a vulnerable position where they often find themselves being attacked as much by other Christians as by the enemy. Even so, many Christian musicians are finding the courage to press beyond the present limits of their time to help prepare the way for a great spiritual advance.

The Path Of Explorers

If we examine the paths historic explorers made while seeking to discover new lands, we will immediately notice that they seldom went in a straight line. Lewis and Clark wandered up numerous box canyons that forced them to frequently backtrack. Spiritual pioneers have likewise seldom followed a perfectly straight course—they will make mistakes. These mistakes which can cost the explorers much time and energy, enable those who follow them to have a much easier journey.

Even the timid and the critical will ultimately benefit from the courage of those who, like Abraham, are willing to leave the security of the known to find out what God is doing. Seeking breakthroughs into new spiritual regions, many have dared to break ranks with the traditional music ministry. They too may make mistakes, but making mistakes is not as deadly as refusing to go up to the promised land and fight when the time comes.

The Wisdom Of Esther

Conservative theologians have historically battled over the canonization of the Book of Esther because God is not even mentioned in it. It is probable that the religious conservatives of Esther's time judged her for becoming the queen in a heathen court, but it was all a part of God's strategy to save her people, which also included those religious conservatives. The Lord could have saved them another way, but He chose this way for His own reasons.

God gave Esther the wisdom to remain quiet about her faith and her heritage until the proper time. God is presently placing many "Esthers" in positions of secular authority and visibility in music and in many other fields. At the proper time they will use those positions to initiate a mighty deliverance and victory for the church. Many Christians whose songs will reach heights on the pop charts will be used as role models for those who would otherwise be looking to those who personify immorality and debauchery. They would never be able to do this if they stayed within the confines dictated by the timid.

The Lord is now placing chosen vessels in strategic positions of visibility from which they will be able to prophesy and help steer this generation toward its ultimate destiny. The ultimate position of the prophetic minstrels is not to just copy the world's style of music and try to do it better while adding Christian lyrics, but to capture the music that the Father loves, which is played in heaven, and transfer it to the earth.

Some of this music will be received through dreams, visions and other prophetic experiences. This music will be loved by the young and the old alike. It will impart peace to the listeners and give them freedom from the fears and pressures of this world just as David was able to do with His harp. This music will be so compelling that those of every possible genre will be drawn to it, and every other style of music, from country to the classics, will be impacted and changed by it.

A Critical Battleground

Music has a significant place in both heaven and in hell. It has been one of the great spiritual battlegrounds of this century and the battle is increasing in intensity. Men and women in this ministry are now being given a divine strategy and wisdom for the battle. These are also being used to mobilize those who are willing to fight this battle, and it will be one of the most important spiritual battlefields of the nineties.

Music was created as a medium for expressing our worship to God. Worship can be motivated by either adoration or fear, but all worship is basically a focus of our attention upon the object of worship. It is this power to focus men that has made music such a force in directing even basic cultural changes. There is yet much for us to understand about this powerful force in the church and the world. The Lord is now moving in the hearts of His leaders to seek this understanding. If we do not learn to utilize music properly, the enemy will continue to fill the vacuum and use it against us.

The Power Of Worship

Along with capturing the attention and arresting the hearts of unbelievers, the coming anointing on music will propel the church to higher realms of worship, which will cause the entire church to more fully abide in the Lord. When the church enters into the higher realms of worship the result will be increased focus, and a power that releases extraordinary spiritual advances. The Lord is going to use music to help take all of the light that we have been given and focus it like a laser. The more focused it is, the more power it will have to cut through any barrier or darkness.

The vision and strategies that the Lord is now giving His church will be put into songs that will help to seal the hearts of the people with those visions. This will not be accomplished just with catchy tunes or lyrics, but with a powerful anointing that will come from the heart of the Lord to grip the innermost being of His people. In all of this we must understand that it is not just the sound, but the anointing. The sound is important, because the harmony of musical sound is meant to be concordant with the tone of the message the Holy Spirit is seeking to convey, but the anointing is more important.

For those who are prepared to handle the power, the Father is going to share with them the music from heaven that He loves. This music will grip men's hearts like no music that has ever been played before. This music will have the power to lift up those who have fallen to the depths of self and idol worship, and to turn their attention back to the Lord. However, this power cannot be entrusted to those who are still caught in the snares of self or idol worship. To receive the highest anointing, minstrels must be healed of the spiritual wounds and insecurities that cause them to fall into self-centeredness.

This great anointing can be perverted, which will only result in a greater depravity and corruption of soul. *Major* changes must be made in the way the church is now stewarding her music ministries before the Lord can give this greater anointing—for our own safety.

Recovering The Ministry

As a part of the preparation for this great battle, the Christian music ministry will come under a severe discipline from the Lord. We are now in a period of time that the Lord has given to allow all of those who are presently committed to Christian music to repent for allowing the ways of the world to take dominion over their ministries. Many of these have been true spiritual pioneers who simply made a wrong turn and need our help and prayers to find the right path again to do what God called them to do. However, those who refuse to repent, or correct their course, will pay a terrible price. It will begin with media exposés that will make the

Christian music industry repulsive to both the world and the church.

Christian music is not meant to be an *industry*, but a *ministry*, and the Lord will recover it. The Lord cannot endorse an industry with the anointing that is coming. Those who have built their life and outreach upon the foundations of the world will go the way of the world if they do not repent. Those who do repent will quickly find their way again, and will be used mightily in the future to keep this ministry on its proper course, having gained discernment from their mistakes.

The present state of the Christian music industry should not be totally blamed on schemers with evil motives. It is largely the result of well meaning people who, seeking to reach the world, opened the door for the world to come flooding in. As the old proverb declares, "The ship in the sea is fine, but the sea in the ship is not!" The sea is now pouring in and this ship will soon go to the bottom. However, the Lord has another ship that will complete His intended journey for music.

What Propels Us?

Isaiah 33:21 reads, **"But there the majestic One, the Lord, shall be for us a place of rivers and wide canals, on which no boat with oars shall go, and on which no mighty ship shall pass" (Isaiah 33:21).** As stated, "Boats with oars" represent ministries that are propelled by human power. "Mighty ships" represent what we might call "megaministries." Neither of these will be allowed when the River of Life begins to flow in these last days.

Paul said, ...**neither is He served by human hands**... (**Acts 17:25**). By our own efforts we can make our ministries move and appear like they are really going somewhere, and we will be, but we will not be going where the Lord would have us to go. Those who appear not to be going anywhere may be closer to the will of God than those who are moving very fast, but by human effort.

During the time of Isaiah, the only other form of propulsion except for oars was the wind. Wind often represents the Spirit in Scripture (John 3:8). Oars were put on ships and boats because when the wind did not blow, or did not blow from the desired direction, they did not want to wait for it. That may be fine for commerce or warships, but for those who serve the Lord. When the Spirit is not moving we must not move either. When we do move we only want to move in the direction that the Spirit is moving. This requires great faith and patience. If we want to inherit the promises of God, and not just waste our lives on what may be good works, but not His works, we must learn to sail with the wind, and be completely dependent upon the Spirit to move us.

"Mighty ships" can be useful on the ocean, but the River of Life is a river, not an ocean. In the day of the Lord's glory He will be a broad river, but not one on which "mighty ships" will be allowed. Even on the broadest rivers, large ships endanger all of the other vessels, blocking or hindering their free movement.

We have been through a period in Western Christianity when we have perceived that the blessings of God upon a ministry were evidenced by their size and rate of growth. The Lord has blessed many of these, and blessed the church and the world through them as much as He could. However, the day is now upon us when being too large will handicap us from being able to continue moving with the Lord in His present purposes.

Because the Lord truly desires for all to be saved and come to the knowledge of the truth, He does love numbers. However, there is a limit to the size where churches and ministries can maintain the maneuverability that will be required for following the Lord in the coming times. To have a hundred churches of a thousand people, or even a thousand churches of a hundred each, will be better than having a single church of a hundred thousand. We must learn to grow in ways that enable us to maintain our flexibility, or we will grow right out of the will of the Lord. Small "ships" and "boats" that are reproducing others are much to be preferred over mighty ones.

Anytime we use such general terms as "mighty" and "small" we must understand that this definition can change with times and places. What might be considered an excessively large church or ministry in one nation may be small in another. I consider Morningstar to be very small, and it is compared to the ministries of some of my friends. However, other friends consider MorningStar a behemoth. I think the key words here are "flexible" and "maneuverable." Can we navigate the course we have been given easily, and without endangering others?

Many churches and ministries grow because they are anointed, and then they lose their anointing trying to sustain a level of growth beyond the level of domain that they have been given. How much of our growth really is because of the anointing and how much is the result of our own promotional skills? It is very possible to out-grow the Lord's purpose in our lives, which may disqual-ify us from the most important commission of all for which He could have otherwise used us.

What Is Success?

All ministries must maintain the prophetic sensitivity to perceive even the smallest change of direction by the Holy Spirit. Contracts, the "business aspects" of being in a "successful" ministry, and other such trappings will disqualify many from being able to flow with the coming move of the Holy Spirit. Now is the time to get rid of excess baggage, trim down, and learn not to measure success by how many records or books are being sold, but by how much more intimate our fellowship is with the Lord.

There is a temporary success available to those who try to build according to the ways of the world. The enemy continues to offer every anointed vessel the world if they will just bow to his ways. This is the way that many do gain the whole world, or the attention of the world, but it will always be short-lived, and it will ultimately end in destruction. There are many promoters who prey upon the selfish ambitions of those who burst upon the scene with a measure of anointing. They can deliver on their promises and have helped many to the top of the Christian music world, or Christian ministry in general. Their motivation usually seems good, like being able to reach more people with the gospel, but if you do it their way you may end up accomplishing much in the name of the Lord, but He will not know you (See Matthew 7:21-23).

This is not at all to imply that all large and visible ministries have grown this way. John the Baptist did not have all Israel coming out to him because of his promotions, neither did Jesus. Neither did the apostle Paul become known throughout the world by self-promotion. Some will gain the visibility of the world because they are anointed. Those who gain influence by the anointing will not have to maintain a huge organization to accomplish their mandate. They will not trust in "horses and chariots," they will trust the Holy Spirit.

Those who choose the way of the Lord must walk in the way of humility, sacrifice and patience to attain the treasures that will last forever. **"Whoever exalts himself shall be humbled; and whoever humbles himself shall be exalted" (Matthew 23:12).** Those who promote themselves seeking quick success God will not promote, but those who humble themselves and walk the way of patience will be anointed and mightily used by God. **"Humble yourselves, therefore, under the mighty hand of God, that He may exalt you at the *proper time"* (I Peter 5:6).**

The Judgment

One reason that such striving has been able to gain a foothold in the church, and especially in many music ministries, is because they have not been given their worthy wages. The church has not looked out for their interests, and the Christian music industry has exploited them. We cannot serve God and mammon, and mammon has become a primary motivation in the Christian music industry. With some this is greed; with others it is simply insecurity and the lack of grace in handling "market forces." The Lord begins judgment with His own house (see I Peter 4:17), and He is about to release a James 5 judgment against the Christian music industry:

Come now, you rich, weep and howl for your miseries which are coming upon you.

Your riches have rotted and your garments have become moth-eaten.

Your gold and your silver have rusted; and their rust will be a witness against you and will consume your flesh like fire. It is in the last days that you have stored up your treasure!

Behold, the pay of the laborers who mowed your fields, and which has been withheld by you, cries out against you; and the outcry of those who did the harvesting has reached the ears of the Lord of Sabaoth.

> **You have lived luxuriously on the earth and led a life of wanton pleasure; you have fattened your hearts in the day of slaughter (James 5:1-5).**

This judgment is partly the result of the laborers not receiving their worthy wages. The world's system that was adopted by much of the Christian music industry robs those with the anointing, such as the songwriters, musicians and singers, so that they are propelled into lifestyles that utterly sap the anointing they were given. Because of this the entire church is robbed of the gift.

The judgment has already begun as the "riches have rotted and your garments have become moth eaten." First, the resources for perpetuating the industry will not just dry up, they will become "rotten." That is, they will come from evil, worldly sources. Because the Lord will remove His grace and anointing, even the most loyal Christian followers will begin to look at the whole of Christian music as a worn out garment that needs to be discarded.

The music and the anointing that the Lord is about to share with those who can receive it does have unprecedented commercial value. With the present system it would be tragically prostituted, and He is not going to trust us with it until we get the process right. We cannot use the world's system of compensation for artists and others, but must seek the Lord's ways, which will promote such equity, justice and grace that it will help to change the world's system.

The first step toward a repentance, that will result in the Lord's endorsement, is to return to our first love—worshipping Him. Because all music promotes worship in some form, if our hearts are not right we will pervert the power of this anointing. Our music must promote the worship of the Father, obedience to the Spirit, and the witness of Jesus.

If the Christian music establishment does not repent, and return to its first love, its lampstand will soon be removed and what light it now has will go out. When we do repent, we will find the greatest desire of our heart, peace, and even greater resources for the extravagant worship of the King. Proverbs 11:24-25 declares: **"There is one who scatters, yet increases all the more, and there is one who withholds what is justly due, but it results only in want. The generous man will be prosperous, and he who waters will himself be watered."**

The anointing that is coming upon the Lord's minstrels is a weapon too powerful to be entrusted to the immature, the impatient, or the self-seeking. Those who have built their ministries upon the ways of the world will soon see them collapse. Those who build upon the proper foundation will be pillars in a mighty new Tabernacle of David that is about to be raised up so that all of the nations may seek the presence of the Lord.

The Church's Responsibility To Minstrels

The whole church has a responsibility to the music ministry. Christian musicians must be recognized as true ministers and they should be spiritually equipped and supported as such. When they go out to minister they should be sent out with prayer and sustained with continual intercession just as any other missionary would be sent out. There is a mighty army of music ministers who are about to be anointed with the prophetic power to capture the attention of a generation. A great opportunity is about to present itself to those who have the foresight and courage to recognize it.

Let us not be timid, but let us be wise and make ourselves utterly dependent upon the presence and anointing of the Lord. Some of the best musicians will not qualify for the new ministry because of their pride and dependence on their natural talents. The Lord will bless a devotion to excellence for His glory, and He accepts the practice of His minstrels as worship, but the anointing of the Holy Spirit is far more valuable than the greatest natural talents. Those who seek the anointing of the Holy Spirit even more than they practice their music, and learn to minister to the Lord with prayer and fasting, have chosen the greater part and will receive it.

Chapter Six

Birthpangs And Earthquakes

The barometer of spiritual intensity in the church is rising around the world. We are now well into a great spiritual advance. There is an increasing anointing for mobilizing the saints for the spreading of the gospel and tearing down strongholds. Walls and barriers between local congregations are being brought down. Everywhere churches are being energized with fresh zeal for the Lord. Genuine tokens of revival are now breaking out around the world.

Earthquakes will accompany these spiritual birth pangs. The events that take place in the natural are often a reflection of the activity occurring in the spiritual realm. Earthquakes are caused when the geological plates begin to shift and move in opposite directions. The very foundations of civilization are beginning to shift and move in opposite directions. The result of this is going to be increasing spiritual and natural earthquakes. However, we have a foundation that cannot be shaken. To the degree that we build our lives on the kingdom of God, we will be protected from the devastation, and will be in a position to help those who are not now protected.

Insurance companies define earthquakes as "acts of God," and they are right. God does not act arbitrarily. The Los Angeles earthquake of January 1994, and the continuing aftershocks, are both signs and judgment.

They are, in fact, the result of the church in Los Angeles coming into a degree of unity and praying for their city.

A primary stronghold over Southern California is the spirit of seduction. *Newsweek* described this target when listing the destruction of this quake: "The studios of virtually every major American producer and distributor of pornographic videos, *an industry that happened to locate itself almost directly atop the fault zone.*" Neither was it an accident that the quake took place at 4:31 a.m. Acts 4:31 reads:

> **"And when they had prayed, the place where they were assembled together was shaken; and they were all filled with the Holy Spirit, and they spoke the word of God with boldness" (NKJV).**

That this event took place at 4:31 a.m. was meant to give greater boldness to the saints for preaching the word, especially the saints in Southern California.

Power Versus Ratings

Southern California has been the seat of one of the most powerful spirits of seduction released in this century. A movie rated PG-13 coming out of Hollywood can have more power to seduce than some "R" or X-rated movies coming out of other places. For this reason we must depend on discernment, not ratings, when we determine what we will watch, or what we will allow our children to watch. It is not the amount of skin that is shown, it is the power behind a movie that counts.

The Lord could shut down all pornography around the world whenever He wants, but He will not do it without the church. He has commissioned us to be the light of the world, and the salt of the earth. He is only waiting for us to come into harmony with His will before He moves. When He determines that the time for judgment has come, He wants His church praying for it, just as Elijah did to get the attention of his nation. Effective prayer has touched the heart of God *for* Southern California and He responded with this earthquake as a sign, and a judgment.

The Lord would always rather show mercy than judgment. Even though He has been showing great mercy to Southern California for this entire century, beginning with the Azuza Street Revival and continuing with the great movements and ministries He presently has based there, His strategy is now moving toward more serious judgments.

There will be more, and increasingly devastating, earthquakes in Southern California. For as long as the church prays the Lord will not relent until there is repentance and change. Repentance and change can spare California. Without it, a major part of that state will be utterly destroyed. Either way, the heart of God has been touched concerning the spirit of seduction that emanates from Southern California and He will not let up until it is removed. Let us pray that the easier way, repentance, is taken.

This is not the time for the church to abandon California, but to labor with even more boldness, which was the message of Acts 4:31. The move of the Holy Spirit over the next few years will be greater than any other witnessed in that state that has seen so much of the glory of God. Los Angeles really can become "the city of angels." San Francisco and San Diego can become great beacons that shine all the way to Asia. Where sin abounds there is even more grace for those who carry the light. This is the time to be bold with the grace and the light.

Spiritual Earthquakes

Along with what is taking place in the natural realm, major spiritual earthquakes are about to take place in the church. Pressure has been building up at certain points in the foundations, and they are about to give way, creating major shock waves. These shifts are going to upset the status quo and result in some serious "structural damage" to the visible church. But only that which can be shaken will be shaken. That which is properly lined up with the true foundations of the faith will not be damaged. When these great spiritual earthquakes are over most of the church will be in much closer harmony with the Lord, and the whole church will be much more stable.

We Are Ambassadors

One point where a great shift is imminent is in the practical application of our ministry as ambassadors of the kingdom. When Paul said, **"We are ambassadors for Christ" (II Corinthians 5:20)**, this was a statement so stunning that it probably buckled the knees of those who read it. In the days of the empire, an ambassador held one of the most esteemed and prestigious positions that one could attain. Because communication between the sending government and its ambassadors could take many months, the ambassadors sometimes were required to make major decisions in the name of their government. This necessitated that the ambassador be able to make agreements that carried the full authority of the emperor. Therefore only those who were considered to be the most loyal and single minded would be chosen for such a position. Paul was saying to the Corinthians that we have been given this same kind of authority to represent the kingdom of God!

Even with the most trusted men in these positions, ambassadors would only be assigned to a country for two or three years before being brought back home. This was because that after even a short time in the host country, there would be a tendency to take on some of the traits of that culture which could make them sympathetic to it. When this happened one might be inclined to serve the interests of the host country more than the one they represented. It is for this same reason that the Lord occasionally shifts His ministers from place to place, or from position to position. These changes help to keep our perspective fresh.

The apostle Paul said, "… **and to the Jews I became as a Jew**… **(I Corinthians 9:20).** There is a sense in which we must try to fit in with those that we have been sent to so that we do not become *unnecessarily* offensive. However, in a general sense, and almost universally,

Christians, churches and even missionaries, have compromised their effectiveness for the kingdom of God because they have become too sympathetic to the spirit of the surrounding culture they are in. To represent the kingdom, and to be effective witnesses, usually requires that we move in an *opposite spirit* to the prevailing spirit of our nation or locality.

The Power Of Difference

One of the most devastating misconceptions to dilute the power of the church's witness to the world is the belief that we can best reach those who are from our own backgrounds. If we come out of a business background, we feel called to reach businessmen. If we are called out of the drug culture, we feel that we can best reach those who we were the most like. This seems reasonable but is often contrary to the Lord's strategy. In His wisdom He sent Peter to the Jews and Paul to the Gentiles.

According to our prevailing philosophy of missions, He should have sent Paul to the Jews. He was a "Pharisee of Pharisees" and certainly they could identify better with him than with Peter. And Peter, being a common fisherman, could certainly fit in better with the Gentiles. But the Lord did not want them to fit in—He wanted them to stick out! Even more, He did not want their witness to depend on the people identifying with them in the flesh; He wanted His messengers to be utterly dependent on the Holy Spirit.

Both Peter and Paul were cast into roles that made them offensive to those to whom they were sent. There was only one way that either of them could accomplish their mission—they had to have the anointing! They were both thrust into utter dependency upon the Holy Spirit, and that is when the Holy Spirit is best able to do His work.

We also see that when Peter left the place of his anointing and tried to go to the Gentiles by visiting Antioch, he got into such serious trouble that Paul had to publicly rebuke him because **"... he stood condemned" (see Galatians 2:11-14).** Likewise, when Paul tried to go to the Jews by visiting Jerusalem, he got into trouble. I submit to you that there was an easier way for Paul to get to Rome, as he was prophetically warned at each stop when he was enroute to Jerusalem. In like manner, many of us stay in trouble in our ministries because we do not remain in the place of our anointing, which is the only place where we will have true spiritual authority.

Sphere Of Authority

It is natural for us to feel more security when we are with those that we are the most like, but this security is not the security of the Holy Spirit. Our flesh wars against the spirit, and if we try to appease the desires of our flesh for security it will have us in conflict with the Holy Spirit. The realm where we have true spiritual authority will usually be in a place that casts us in utter dependency upon the Holy Spirit, which will always make us insecure in our flesh.

Paul recognized a sphere of authority that he had been given and did not want to presume to go beyond it (see II Corinthians 10:13-15). Just as a policeman in Atlanta does not have authority in Amsterdam, we must learn to stay within the realms that we have been appointed to if we are to be effective.

This principle does not just relate to geography, but is spiritual as well. Many prophets have fallen from grace because they tried to become teachers, just as many teachers have fallen from grace because they have tried to become prophets. Many evangelists have fallen because they tried to become pastors, and vice versa. This is not to negate the fact that some have dual, or even multiple callings, but we must never presume to go beyond our appointed sphere.

When we try too hard to be like those we are sent to we are compromising our position of spiritual authority which often requires us to move in an opposite spirit to that which prevails in the land. This does not mean that we should purposely try to be different in everything. Our authority is not in being different, but in the Holy Spirit. We simply will be different if we abide in Him and are true to the work He is accomplishing in us. The Lord Jesus stated it well:

You are those who justify yourselves in the sight of men, but God knows your hearts; for

> **that which is highly esteemed among men** *is*
> **detestable in the sight of God (Luke 16:15).**

If we are compelled to do the things that will make us acceptable to men we will be doing what is detestable to God. The reverse is also true; the things that are highly esteemed with God are detestable in the sight of men. Somebody is going to detest what we are doing. Who do we want it to be?

The church in general, and even many missionaries, have embraced "the spirit of the land" to the degree that we cannot properly represent the Lord and His kingdom. The Holy Spirit is now bringing conviction upon the church in this area, which is essential before we can receive the authority that we need for this time. Those who begin to change their direction in this will create opposition in the world, but will regain the favor of God. Those who do not repent will have it easier for a short time, but they will ultimately have a much more difficult time. Repentance in this area will ultimately deliver the church from the dependency on artificial props and devices for witnessing to men in place of the Holy Spirit.

The Fear Of God

To properly represent the kingdom of God, we must fear God more than we fear men. One of the great biblical statements which sums up what is required of a true ambassador was made by Elijah. In what appears to be his first public prophecy, made before the king of his nation, he declares: **"As the Lord God of Israel lives,** *before whom I stand*, **there shall not be dew nor rain these years, except at my word"** (I Kings 17:1 NKJV). By this statement he was declaring to Ahab that he was not standing before him—he was just a king, just a man. Elijah did not live his life before men, even the most prestigious of men, but before God.

For the church to accomplish her mandate for this hour she will need the kind of authority that Elijah walked in, and more. Before we can be trusted with this we must be delivered from the fear of man and live only in the pure and holy fear of God.

To lead men into a true conversion we do not want them to feel comfortable with us and our message, but very uncomfortable! For true conversion men must be convicted of their ways that are in contrast with God's ways. Paul said, **"If I were still trying to please men *I would not be a bondservant of Christ"* (Galatians 1:10).** Paul acknowledged that his flesh had been a trial to the Galatians (see Galatians 4:13). This required them to either be repelled by him, or receive him as "an angel of God," which they did. When men are attracted to the gospel because they are attracted to us, we should seriously wonder about both the state of our lives and the gospel we are preaching.

The Lord Jesus said, **"How can you believe, when you receive glory from one another, and you do not seek the glory that is from the one and only God?"** (John 5:44). The Greek word that is translated "glory" in this text is *doxa*, which could have been translated "recognition." By this statement the Lord was declaring that we lose our faith when we seek glory or recognition from men. Faith comes from our focus upon, and recognition of, who Jesus is. When we become more concerned with what men think of us than what God thinks of us we are falling from the faith.

How much of what we are building and doing in our ministries is for the purpose of attracting people? It is not hard to attract multitudes of people through hype and manipulation. True spiritual success cannot be measured by how many people we attract, but by our ability to attract God. God does care about numbers—He desires to see all men saved. When we begin to build churches by being more concerned about what attracts God than what attracts people, we will end up attracting many more people than we do now. When Jesus is truly lifted up He will draw more people than our best programs.

The Foundational "Plates" Of The Church Are Shifting

The people who are drawn to Jesus will also come through a true conversion. Those who come to Jesus through true conversion will not be the "high maintenance, lowimpact" people who now fill many churches. Even with the breakup of the Soviet Union, the "meet my need" spirit of socialism continues to advance in the world. This same mentality, which is nothing less than "spiritual socialism," now dominates much of the church. These foundational pressures that have built up within the church are moving in the opposite direction of the work of the Holy Spirit in the church, and a major spiritual earthquake is now looming because of it.

The Lord does want to meet people's needs, and He is obviously the best at this, but He does not meet them in a way that only feeds our self-centeredness. The church in the West is almost completely unprepared for difficulties, and we are entering the time of great trouble. The Lord is going to build a church that actually thrives on opposition and trouble. His people will look at the greatest of difficulties just like Joshua and Caleb looked at the giants in the Promised Land, declaring that, "They will be bread for us!"

As the Lord establishes His foundation in the church it will often be moving in the opposite direction of the foundational movements in society, resulting in the greatest confrontation between the church and the social order since the first century A.D. The power behind the foundational movements in the church is the irresistible power of God, and the church will prevail. The resulting earthquakes will be devastating to all who are going in the wrong direction.

Holiness Will Prevail Over Seduction

The power of the church in California to overcome the powers of darkness is to embrace the cross and walk in holiness before the Lord. Because of many legalistic extremes, and a satanic strategy to devalue its importance, "holiness" has become a repulsive word throughout much of the body of Christ, especially in California. This has caused many believers to succumb more to the spirit of the age than to the Spirit of Christ. Some have drifted into infidelity, licentiousness, or a lukewarmness that is tolerant of the gross darkness. We must acknowledge that this gross darkness has been released upon the land during our watch. The alarm must now be sounded, but we can hardly sound the alarm against the enemy if we are of one mind with him!

There is a call upon the church in California to recapture the essence of true holiness. There is a special anointing on the church in California for leadership. When this is not used for the timely purposes of the Lord, it is diverted by the enemy and used to promote evil trends in both the church and society (whatever is loosed in heaven is also loosed upon the earth). The ability of the church to fulfill her calling is dependent upon our attachment to the Holy Spirit, and He is first and foremost *HOLY!*

Isaiah 52 is filled with wisdom concerning this call to holiness. Though it is a specific word for California it certainly has relevance for all believers.

> **Awake, awake! Put on your strength, O Zion; put on your beautiful garments, O Jerusalem, the *holy* city! For the uncircumcised and the unclean shall no longer come to you (NKJV).**

The strength of the church in California will be her purity and cleanliness of spirit. Those who join themselves to the church will be truly born again and circumcised of heart.

Shake yourself from the dust, rise up O captive Jerusalem; Loose yourself from the chains around your neck, O captive daughter of Zion.

Because Adam was made from the dust it often speaks of the flesh—the shakings are meant to awaken the church and move her to put off her carnal ways. It is now time to cast off the deeds of the flesh, and the yokes that men have placed upon us, and take our stand with boldness.

For thus says the Lord, "You were sold for nothing and you will be redeemed without money."

Money and other such resources will not be the source of our redemption or victory. We must cast off the financial considerations as primary motives in decision making and submit to the Holy Spirit.

For thus says the Lord God, "My people went down at the first into Egypt to reside there, then the Assyrian oppressed them without cause.

The bondage of Israel came two ways: she went down to Egypt voluntarily which resulted in bondage, and she was allowed to be attacked by Assyria because she had fallen into apostasy ("without cause" implies that it did not have to happen). Likewise, the present bondage of the church is the result of her having drifted into the ways of the world (Egypt), and in some cases, having fallen into apostasy by worshipping other gods such as prestige (typified by worship on the high places), money (golden calves), personalities (Asherah), manipulation (Baal), humanism (gods made by human hands), etc.. Almost every church has subtly fallen into the worship of the "other gods" to at least some degree and we must remove them from our midst.

> **"Now therefore, what do I have here," declares the Lord, "seeing that My people have been taken away without cause?" Again the Lord declares, "Those who rule over them howl, and My name is continually blasphemed all day long.**

> **"Therefore My people shall know My name; therefore in that day I am the One who is speaking, 'Here I am.'"**

The Lord has taken notice of the blaspheming of the heathen because of the condition of His church, and because of this His people are about to know His authority (name). The Lord is speaking to His people now saying, "Here I am." He does not want to remain distant; He wants to be found by His people. We can all be as close to Him as we want to be.

> **How lovely on the mountains are the feet of him who brings good news, who announces peace and brings good news of happiness, who announces salvation, and says to Zion, "Your God reigns!"**

Mountains speak of governments or powers and the church is about to impact them with the good news of the gospel (not politics). With this gospel will come peace, joy (happiness) and salvation. With this the reign of God will begin to be proclaimed, and believed.

Your watchmen lift up their voices, with their voices they shall sing together; for they shall see eye to eye when the Lord turns back Zion (NKJV).

Watchmen were one of the designations for prophets in the Old Testament. Here the Lord is promising the lifting up of prophetic voices. This lifting up is the result of the unity that they will come into (singing together and seeing "eye to eye").

Break forth, shout joyfully together, you waste places of Jerusalem; for the Lord has comforted His people, He has redeemed Jerusalem.

After the watchmen come into unity the whole church will break forth and "shout together," which includes the bringing forth of a common message. With this unity there will be great peace and comfort, regardless of the times.

The Lord has bared His holy arm in the sight of all the nations, that all the ends of the earth may see the salvation of our God.

The "arm of the Lord" always speaks of His strength. It should be noted here that His arm is "holy." There is a strength that will be revealed when His body begins to walk in a holiness that will be revealed in the sight of all nations. This will make His salvation clear to all nations.

> **Depart, depart, go out from there, touch nothing unclean; go out of the midst of her, purify yourselves, you who carry the vessels of the Lord.**

This is another exhortation to maintain the holiness that is befitting of the church of Jesus Christ. Repetition of this theme is meant to emphasize its critical importance.

> **But you will not go out in haste, nor will you go as fugitives; for the Lord will go before you, and the God of Israel will be your rear guard.**

Regardless of troubles of the times, or persecutions, the church will not go on the defensive and become fugitives, but as the first verse declares, we must "Rise up!" The Lord will be the One who backs us up; He will be our Rear Guard.

> **Behold, My servant will prosper, He will be high and lifted up, and greatly exalted.**

During the time of the greatest trouble in the world, the breaking of the nations and almost universal poverty, the church will know prosperity and the Lord Jesus will be greatly exalted.

> **Just as many were astonished at you, My people, so His appearance was marred more than any man, and His form more than the sons of men.**

The historic humiliation of the church was allowed so that we can identify with the Lord in His humiliation.

Like Him, the church is also destined for a great exaltation, but we must never forget that it is by His grace.

Thus He will sprinkle many nations, kings will shut their mouths on account of Him; for what had not been told them they will see, and what they had not heard they will understand.

The Lord Jesus is about to touch all nations with the power of His blood. The coming exaltation of Jesus will be so great that even those who have not heard the gospel presented clearly will understand it. **"Where sin abounded, grace did much more abound" (Romans 5:20 KJV),** and during this coming time of great darkness, the glory of the Lord will shine brighter than ever.

Rise Up

The retreat of the church has reached its limit. Now the advance will begin. It will gain momentum until the whole world takes notice. She will march resolutely to the field of battle. The ultimate conflict between light and darkness is now upon us. It is time to put on our strength, true holiness, as the arm of the Lord is about to be revealed. Even nature will quake and shudder as a witness that the foundations of heaven and earth are moving in *opposite* directions. But our God will prevail, and our victory is assured. This is the time to be bold as we have never been bold before. There is no turning back!

Chapter Seven

The War

Satan's ultimate goal is to populate hell. His greatest ally for accomplishing this goal is death. His most effective means for bringing about death is war. Instigating war in any form, between anyone that he can get to fight, is one of his most basic strategies against mankind. He views every war as a victory, and the most destructive ones as some of his greatest achievements. Just as Jesus is the Prince of Peace, Satan is the Prince of War.

There are "righteous wars" which are fought for righteous causes. Even so, every war should be viewed by the church as a significant defeat, even if the cause of righteousness prevails. They are defeats because the Lord has invested in the church an authority for waging spiritual warfare which, if exercised properly, can accomplish the goals of righteous causes without the destruction of war.

It is Satan's strategy to bring every human conflict to a violent confrontation, which results in as much death and destruction as possible. Just as Jesus was sent to destroy the works of the devil, we have been sent into the world with this same commission. As one of Satan's ultimate goals is to spread death by war, believers are sent forth as peacemakers to thwart this strategy.

The church must go to war against the enemy's basic strategy of war. This ultimate conflict between life and death is about to enter its last and greatest battle. It will rage from one end of the earth to the other, in every city and town, on every social, philosophical, and political front. A time is coming when every debate, every political campaign, every social movement, will be seen as a battle line between these ultimate spiritual forces. There will be no neutral ground, no truces, no peace in this war. This will be both the most dangerous and the most opportune time for Christianity since the beginning.

Fight For Life

The ultimate goal of the church is to populate heaven. Our ultimate weapon is the gospel of salvation—the words of everlasting life. The church is about to be given the words of life with greatly increased power. These words will be spiritual bombs and hand grenades with the power to destroy even the most effective strongholds of the enemy. Individual statements spoken by Christians will be able to unravel the intricate webs of deception that the enemy has taken years to weave. Single public statements by Christians will invalidate the enemy's propaganda built upon multiplied thousands of books, articles and public statements over many years of time.

This power in words will not be gained cheaply. Those who are given this authority will be those who have faithfully waged their own war against their own tongues, bringing them into submission to the Holy Spirit. They will have spent years waging war against their own wayward thoughts, bringing them all under subjection to Christ. Pure waters must come from pure wells. The purity of our own lives will dictate whether or not the waters of life can flow through us, as is written: **"Watch over your heart with all diligence, for from it flow the springs of life"** (Proverbs 4:23).

The Weapons Of This War

Solomon declared: **"Death and life are in the power of the tongue, and those who love it will eat its fruit"** (Proverbs 18:21). Every word that we speak can have the power to impart faith or fear, peace or strife, joy or gloom, love or hatred; and we ourselves will eat the fruit of our words. We must heed the apostle's warning, **"Do not be deceived, God is not mocked; for whatever a man sows, this he will also reap"** (Galatians 6:7). Are our words spreading the light of the kingdom of God, or the darkness of this present evil age?

Because **"out of the abundance of the heart the mouth speaks"** (Matthew 12:34 NKJV), our words reveal either the light or the corruption that is in our hearts. The apostle Paul exhorts us in II Corinthians 13:5: **"Test yourselves to see if you are in the faith; examine yourselves! Or do you not recognize this about yourselves, that Jesus Christ is in you—unless indeed you fail the test."** How can we test ourselves to see if Jesus is in us? By testing our conversation. Is Jesus in our words?

Our words and our conversation reflect what is in our hearts. If Jesus truly lives in us He should be the primary subject of our conversation. If we spend more time talking about movies, sports, even the news and current events, than we do about Jesus, it should be a sign to us that we are failing the most important test that we can ever take. Whatever in our lives eclipses Jesus as the focus of our conversation, has eclipsed Him as the focus of our hearts, and has become an idol taking His place.

Not only does our conversation reflect what is in our heart, but if Jesus truly rules in our hearts He should be the One who controls our tongues. The ultimate goal of every Christian should be not only to love Him above all else, but to be controlled by Him. Our ultimate goal should be to only speak words that are prompted by the Spirit, that reflect the heart of God, and reveal the light of the Savior in this dark world. This should not just be the goal of prophets, but every Christian. We are all called to abide in Him and manifest the sweet aroma of the knowledge of Him in every place.

Regardless of our vocation, whether we are the president or a plumber, our highest calling in this life is to be an ambassador for the King of Kings—to speak what is on His mind, to do what He would do in every situation. This is the reason why we are on this earth. There is nothing higher or more important that we can do than this. It is just as important that we reveal Him regardless of whether we are speaking to the president or to a plumber—the Lord shows no partiality.

The most important man who ever lived was a carpenter, and to that Carpenter some of the most important men alive are still in the lowest professions. A common laborer who is noble of spirit, who abides in Christ, can have more power to impact this world than a president. **"God has chosen the foolish things of the world to shame the wise, and God has chosen the weak things of the world to shame the things that are strong" (I Corinthians 1:27).** Regardless of what we do or our position in this world, we can be one of the greatest generals in the most important war ever fought—the war between life and death!

The Battlefield

Now is the time to choose which side we are going to be on in this war. Then we must choose each day to fight with all of our hearts. Every warrior in this battle is given positions to defend and positions to take from the enemy. We must defend our families, our congregations, our offices or places of work, against the words of death, while working each day to extend the domain of the kingdom.

Our battle maps are our prayer lists. We must have specific targets. We must **"box in such a way, as not beating the air" (I Corinthians 9:26),** but know what we are hitting. As we gain dominion over the smaller assignments we will be given more authority to go after major strongholds. Those who take spiritual dominion over their families will then be given their neighbors and their families. Those who take their neighborhoods will then be given their cities to fight for.

In this we must be careful to fight in the areas that we have been assigned and not to go beyond them. Many are trying to take their cities while they have forgotten their families, or churches. In this way we leave the enemy in our rear, where he will ambush us sooner or later.

This does not mean that we should not pray for neighbors or cities until our families have been completely won to Christ, but we must be careful to stay within the realm of our appointed authority. This way we will not be assuming assignments that God has given to others, which will always work to dilute our authority in the area where He has given us a commission. Joel described well the "last day" army of the Lord:

> **They run like might men; they climb the wall like soldiers; and they each march in line, nor do they deviate from their paths.**

> **They do not crowd each other; they march everyone in his path. When they burst through the defenses, they do not break ranks (Joel 2:7-8).**

It is imperative that Christians begin to see every encounter with others as an opportunity to sow life. This does not mean that we must declare the plan of salvation to every checkout clerk or waitress, but we must continually take a stand for the kingdom of God by resolutely maintaining our position in Christ. This position is always demonstrated by the fruit of the Spirit. When we are able to endure the often trying and unfair encounters of life without compromising our position in the love, joy, peace, patience, kindness, goodness, faithfulness, gentleness, self-control, we are extending the limits of the kingdom of God.

If we are going to abide in the Holy Spirit we must see every encounter and every situation from the perspective of heaven's interests. The interests of the kingdom of God will often be contrary to our own human interests. We must abide in the continual understanding that walking as soldiers of the cross demands that we take up our own crosses everyday. Heaven's interest are sometimes best served when our rights are violated and we endure it patiently, even as the Lord Jesus gave us an example on the His cross.

The world is not fair, and no one can expect to be treated fairly all of the time. What we can expect is that when we are treated unfairly, if we maintain our position in the Holy Spirit, He will use the situation for the good of the kingdom. Just as the greatest injustice ever suffered, the crucifixion of Jesus, resulted in the greatest impartation of life, every time we take up our crosses and endure injustice, life is released. The apostle Paul explained this in II Corinthians 4:7-11, 17-18:

But we have this treasure in earthen vessels, that the surpassing greatness of the power may be of God and not from ourselves;

we are afflicted in every way, but not crushed; perplexed, but not despairing;

persecuted, but not forsaken; struck down, but not destroyed;

always carrying about in the body the dying of Jesus, that the life of Jesus also may be manifested in our body.

For we who live are constantly being delivered over to death for Jesus' sake, that the life of Jesus also may be manifested in our mortal flesh.

For momentary, light affliction is producing for us an eternal weight of glory far beyond all comparison,

while we look not at the things which are seen, but at the things which are not seen; for the things which are seen are temporal, but the things which are not seen are eternal.

Troubles are opportunities. The greater the troubles the greater the opportunities. There are no troubles that are too difficult for God. Regardless of what comes against us, we can say with Paul, "… **thanks be to God, who always leads us in His triumph in Christ, and manifests through us the sweet aroma of the knowledge of Him in every place"** (II Corinthians 2:14). Victory is assured! All that we must do to see the victory is to abide in Christ who has already won it, and marvel at the wisdom of how He works it out. When we begin to view trials as important confrontations with the enemy in which ground can be won from him, we will begin to count our trials as joy. The more victories that we see the more joy that they will bring to us. However, we must never settle for anything less than victory and witnessing the sweet knowledge of Jesus prevailing through it.

Be Gentle As Doves Yet Wise As Serpents

Victory is assured if we do not abandon our position in the Holy Spirit. This does not mean that we must always abandon our rights in such matters as business transactions in which we are being defrauded, or in other situations in which we are being taken wrongful advantage of. It may be right for us to maintain our position and demand compliance with agreements, even through lawsuits. Paul's admonition was not to go to court with a brother, but that Christians should be able to decide cases through the authorities in the church. It is true that we will not be fit to judge the world if we cannot decide disputes among ourselves. However, in our dealings with the world there will be times when we should maintain our position and defend our rights through the entire process of the law. However, to do this we must also maintain our position of love, joy, peace, patience, etc., always knowing that even saving one soul for the kingdom is worth the price of being defrauded for any amount.

We must not let anything ever cause us to compromise our position in the kingdom. Even if we win the largest lawsuit by abandoning our position in the fruit of the Spirit, which is to abandon our position in Christ, we will suffer the greater loss. We must view every situation or trial as an opportunity to extend the kingdom, being always ready to testify of the hope that we have.

Being the light of the world, or being the light in a situation, may not involve declaring the gospel. Sometimes we are called to be the light just by doing what is right, and demonstrating a Spirit that is contrary to the spirit of the world. Such are true demonstrations of the kingdom. Such demonstrate the rules of another realm where the fruit of the Spirit prevails.

A Demonstration Of The Kingdom

One of the greatest demonstrations of the Spirit that I have ever witnessed was not a miracle—it was the demonstration of a profound peace and thoughtfulness in an airline ticket line. Because of problems with incoming flights and other delays, the line to one connection had grown to many more people than could be processed in the short time before the flight was to depart. Strife and impatience were rising to the point where I seriously thought that it was going to get out of control.

At the worst possible moment, just after more bad news had been announced, two large, boisterous women, each carrying two large suitcases, started pushing their way through the line demanding to go to the front. I do not recall ever witnessing more obnoxious attitudes in anyone, much less in a situation like this. I was watching, fully expecting someone to deck them both. Then, to my dismay they headed right toward my friend who was in line for the flight. As the clamor behind him grew, he turned to see what was happening.

As others were actually beginning to jostle the two women, my friend instinctively raced to their assistance, asking if he could help them with their bags, and offering them his own position near the front of the line. This action was so contrary to the prevailing spirit in that place that it stunned everyone. A great quiet came over the entire scene. I looked around and almost everyone was staring at my friend with obvious amazement. As he picked up his own bags and moved to the back of the line it seemed that every eye was on him. The two women seemed undone by the unexpected, and unquestionably undeserved, kindness. A powerful peace came over the entire line.

The agents, who had also witnessed the scene, suddenly became agreeable and somehow the flight was delayed enough to get everyone on it. I have witnessed many miracles, but that airport scene still stands out to me as one of the greatest demonstrations of the kingdom I have ever witnessed. As hell was fast gaining control of a volatile situation, and moving it towards potentially serious strife, it seemed that Satan brought in two of his biggest guns in the form of a couple of very ill mannered women, aimed them right at the Christian, who quickly and easily disarmed the enemy and his entire host with one genuine act of kindness.

We have been given this same power, in every situation. When strife arises in our family or at the office, we can join the side of the enemy or the side of the Lord. Who gains the victory in that situation will almost certainly be determined by our choice. If we join the Lord it does not matter if anyone else joins Him with us. One person and the Lord always makes a majority. If we allow the fruit of the Spirit to prevail in us, He will ultimately prevail in any situation we find ourselves.

Summary

Paul said that "...**the God of *peace* will soon crush Satan under your feet**" (Romans 16:20). It is significant that he said that it was the "God of peace" and not "the Lord of hosts" (Lord of armies) that crushes Satan. One person who abides in the peace of God has more power than armies. Solomon stated it well: **"He who is slow to anger is better than the mighty, and he who rules his spirit, than he who captures a city" (Proverbs 16:32).**

We are in a war. This war will not stop just because we decide we do not want to fight anymore. Everyone of us is in a fight to the death. Until death is defeated the fight is not over, for any of us. If we try to back out we will only open ourselves up to a greater onslaught. However, the more we fight the more peace we will know. The peace that we can have by fighting is greater than any peace that the world can know.

We must start to realize every day when we wake up that by the time we lay down again we will have either taken ground from the enemy, or he will have taken ground from us. Why not make the best of it and go after all of the spoil that we can?

The Lord is about to impart a divine militancy to His people so that they are going to wake up every day looking for a fight, but for all of the right reasons. We are about to discover the power of the weapons that we have been given. There is no army in the world that has an arsenal more powerful than that which the Lord has put at the disposal of even His youngest believer. As we discover the power of these weapons the whole world is going to wake up to the nature of the true battle. The whole world will soon be brought to the Valley of Decision.

The ultimate battle at the end of the age will not be fought over abortion, or homosexuality, or any other single moral issue. The battle is much greater than any of these. The battle is between life and death itself. This does not mean that we should not take stands against these issues, but we must see beyond them or we will continue to flail at the branches instead of putting the ax to the root of the tree.

We must understand both the true nature of the battle and the nature of our weapons if we are going to prevail in war. We may have the power to demonstrate, but what we really need are demonstrations of power.

For though we walk in the flesh, we do not war according to the flesh,

for the weapons of our warfare are not of the flesh, but divinely powerful for the destruction of fortresses.

> We are destroying speculations and every lofty
> thing raised up against the knowledge of God,
> and we are taking every thought captive to the
> obedience of Christ,
>
> and we are ready to punish all disobedience,
> whenever your obedience is complete
> (II Corinthians 10:3-6).

It is a primary strategy of the enemy to get us to fight with carnal weapons. He knows that when we do we have crossed over to the dark side, and regardless of what we are fighting for, we are aiding him in the battle. Many of his agents, who come as "angels of light," are zealots and fanatics. Most of them are sincere, but they are zealots and fanatics whose tactics are to use carnal weapons, intimidation and political pressures to try to accomplish their agendas *which are indeed righteous*. Those who succumb to their pressures and intimidations, and join their strategies, will pay a most terrible price, and it will not be for the sake of righteousness or the advancement of the kingdom.

Satan will never cast out Satan. Murder will not cast out abortion, anger will not cast out rebellion, hatred will never cast out immorality. The Lord Jesus affirmed this saying, **"But if I cast out demons by the Spirit of God, then the kingdom of God has come upon you"** (Matthew 12:28).

Paul also instructed:

> Never pay back evil for evil *to anyone*. Respect
> what is right in the sight of all men.

If possible, so far as it depends on you, be at peace with all men.

Never take your own revenge, beloved, but leave room for the wrath of God, for it is written, "Vengeance is Mine, I will repay," says the Lord.

But if your enemy is hungry, feed him, and if he is thirsty, give him a drink; for in so doing you will heap burning coals upon his head.

DO NOT BE OVERCOME BY EVIL, BUT OVERCOME EVIL WITH GOOD (Romans 12:17-21).

Chapter Eight

The Judgment Of War

The testimony of prophecy in Scripture is clear that the last days will be the greatest time of trouble the world has ever known. However, it is also clear that, for those who live by the word of God, it will be their finest hour. This is not a day to fear for those who are prepared. Those who have carefully built their houses upon the Rock never need to fear the storms. Even so, this is not just a time to stand and endure the times and preserve our own houses, but this is the time for the greatest advance of the gospel in history. This is the time when the church will rise up to battle for the eternal destiny of every human soul.

There are wars that are inevitable. Some are the judgment of God over a nation or situation. Even so, they must also be viewed as a defeat for the church, as our failure to bring forth the repentance that could have prevented them. As wars are the ultimate release of death, evil and corruption of the human soul, they usually only occur when the "salt has lost its saltiness."

War is one of the most cruel and devastating judgments. When King David was asked to choose between plagues or war as punishment for numbering Israel, he was wise to choose the plague. There is hardly a greater devastation than when armies pass through a region, raping, pillaging, plundering and destroying. The destructive potential of modern wars is much greater now than in the times of David. In addition, this destructive potential threatens to be released with increasing frequency.

The Diversity Of Conflicts

There will also be different kinds of wars arising as we approach the end of this age. Many of the coming wars will be civil wars fought within the boundaries of single nations, and even cities. Most of these conflicts will be cultural or ethnic, but many others will be fought between idealogies, religions, and political interests. These will consume some nations like a nuclear meltdown from within.

Gang and drug wars will become far more devastating with the distribution of advanced and powerful weapons to these groups. Some gangs numbering in the hundreds will carry the firepower of armies of thousands just a century ago, and they will use it with devastating results. At times whole cities will be abandoned or destroyed by gangs. In some places organized crime will be the only keepers of the peace. War lords will be the only authorities capable of controlling the people.

As the spiritual war between life and death rages, natural wars of all kinds will steadily increase, spreading in some regions like wildfires leaping over national boundaries as if they did not exist. There will be a time when there will seem to be no place on earth that is safe from war in some form. Neighbors from different cultures, who have gotten along well for long periods of time, will wake up as deadly enemies overnight. These outbursts will usually be instigated by irritation arising over seemingly insignificant events between individuals or groups. In reality they result from very old cultural wounds which have never been healed.

The ruthlessness of these outbursts of deadly fury will shock the world. These conflicts will cause people to begin forming tight cloisters with seemingly impregnable walls separating them from other groups. Suspicion of everyone who is different will grow into a gripping paranoia. This will result in a greater fracturing of humanity than has been known since the Tower of Babel.

It is one of the basic strategies of the enemy to make life as cheap as possible. His goal is to make death so common that it becomes increasingly tolerated as a means for settling even petty disputes. Satan wants to make it acceptable to settle with murder the conflicts that used to be resolved with an argument, or at most a fistfight. Then he will push these limits to the point where no dispute is fully settled until the rival's family and associates are also killed. Again, his most basic strategy in this last hour will be to spread as much death as he possible can.

Rwanda—An Example

The recent devastation of Rwanda is an example of the type of conflict that will become increasingly commonplace. Without warning this nation disintegrated into one of the most cruel killing fields of the century—at this writing nearly a million people are thought to have been slaughtered. Survivors have been driven into refugee camps where disease is taking many more lives.

The conflict in Rwanda was the result of spontaneous combustion from smoldering racial fires. Amazingly, the battle was actually fought between two tribes whose greatest distinguishing characteristic was that one tribe tended to be a little taller than the other, and had been politically and economically dominant for a time. This will be the nature of many deadly conflicts—even the smallest of real or perceived differences will be exacerbated until it becomes reason enough to kill for.

When Jesus was asked about the signs of the last days He immediately stated that **"…nation will rise against nation…" (Matthew 24:7).** The Greek word that is translated "nation" here is *ethnos*. This could have been more accurately translated as *"race shall rise against race."* This is precisely the kind of conflicts that are erupting around the world at this time.

Missionaries stationed in Rwanda testified that those people were some of the most gentle and peaceful that they had ever known, but "overnight they became demons." One news correspondent kept repeating that "There is something in their eyes that was not there yesterday." There was! Satan is now being displaced from the heavenly places, and when that happens he comes to the earth with "great wrath." He is now exploiting to the fullest degree every open door that he has into

140

the affairs of men, and his greatest open door is the division between races.

The Place Of Safety

It is not in Satan's character to play fair or to honor codes of conduct. He is the father of lies and those who are under his control will use lies as tools for doing their deadly work. They will seem to possess the best of intentions, but will make treaties and agreements that they have no intention of keeping. The most ruthless and cruel rule of naked power will emerge as the only source of earthly authority. Those who do try to live by a humanistic code of honor will become increasingly vulnerable in these times. Codes of honor and standards of integrity will mean nothing to those who attain dominion by force.

Even so, true spiritual authority is greater than any power on earth. Christians who abide in Christ will have more authority than the powers of this evil age. However, this will be the time when true spiritual power will seem to be the most impotent. Only those whose spiritual eyes are opened to perceive the true nature of events will understand that the opposite is, in fact, true. We must not fall into the snare of trying to compete in the realm of earthly power. Those who are guilty of exerting influence according to the power of the carnal weapons and politics of this world will enter a realm where they have no authority, and no protection.

Daniel foresaw this time of trouble: **"I kept looking, and that horn was waging war with the saints and overpowering them until the Ancient of Days came, and judgment was passed in favor of the saints of the Highest One, and the time arrived when the saints took possession of the kingdom" (Daniel 7:21-22).** One of the most treacherous and devastating deceptions promulgated has been the belief that the church is called now to assume civil authority. We only stand by the grace of God, and when we try to assume authority prematurely we depart from the place of God's present grace for us. To seek civil authority before the Lord comes, and before the ordained "time" for the saints to take possession of the kingdom, is to be lured into the special domain of Satan, without the protection of God's grace. Historically this has resulted in some of history's greatest tragedies, and this will continue to until the time fully arrives, which we will know by the coming of the Lord.

When we are cast into the inevitable confrontations with those who rule by carnal power, we must not try to gain influence or advantage by any means other than the truth that Jesus Christ is the Lord of the nations. The only authority that we will have is truth, but truth is more powerful than lies. Those who live by truth and take their stand on truth will ultimately prevail over those who receive their authority from the father of lies. If we stand on the truth we will prevail even if we die, as our deaths will have more power than the influence of all who continue in the earthly realm. It is better to die with integrity than to live with dishonor.

The victory of the saints in this hour will be that **"They overcame him because of the blood of the Lamb and because of the word of their testimony, and they did not love their life even to death" (Revelation 12:11).** Those who have embraced the cross have already died to this world; and those who have died to this world cannot be influenced by the fear of death. Those who cannot be affected by the fear of death will stand out as the brightest lights in a world gripped with the darkness of paranoia. Those who know their God, and know the paradise to which death in this world delivers them, will live in greater peace of heart during this time than when the world was in the time of relative stability.

A Nation Within Nations

The common thread that links all human beings together will become very thin and fragile, but the Lord will anoint peacemakers in every culture to keep it from completely dissolving. These peacemakers will be Christians who have become true ambassadors of the kingdom of God.

In the midst of this great evaporation of civilization, the church will arise as a "nation" that is composed of those from every nation. The church will ultimately become the one common denominator in the world through which the different cultures and races can still relate to each other. Just as on the Day of Pentecost, those from every nation will be able to understand the heavenly language of the church, which will astound and capture the world's attention.

Ultimately the unity of the church in the midst of such worldwide discord will be the marvel of the world, and the greatest testimony ever of the Lordship of Jesus. However, this power will be very subtle at first. It will touch hearts deeply but few will even discuss what they are pondering in their hearts because of their fears. *Gradually* this power of unity will increase in influence until the hope that it presents is stronger than the fears of men. This is because the true unity will grow gradually. As the church grows in unity she will grow in spiritual authority, which is founded upon love. As this spiritual authority, rooted in love, grows, its authority to cast out fear will likewise grow.

The Army Of The Lord

As the spirit of antichrist is rising with its greatest determination to take dominion over the nations, the "nation within the nations" will also have its own army, which will be equally aggressive. World conquest will be her goal. She will never flee from battles, but will seek them with great zeal. This is the hour when the church will arise as never before to aggressively attack every stronghold of the enemy. A divine militancy is coming upon the church that will strike gripping fear into the heart of every power of darkness. This is the time when the church will come into the greatest discipline and authority she has ever known.

The church will not abandon the world in defeat, fleeing when her light is needed the most. She is about to rise to her full spiritual stature. Because the church will be free of the fear of death, or anything else that the world can do to her, the resolve and courage she displays will by themselves conquer whole regions. The Spirit that the church lives by will be her divinely powerful weapons of war, and they will devastate the powers of darkness in every confrontation.

The nature of The Army of the Lord will be different than that of any army that has ever marched—she will wage war by doing good. As earthly armies spread unprecedented devastation in their wake, the army of the Lord will leave restoration, healing, peace and even prosperity in her wake. The world will be a desert before her, and a paradise after she passes. This army will not pillage, plunder and destroy; she will give, build and restore.

The love that is to be revealed in the saints will be so profound that in the time of greatest darkness they will love every minute of every day. They will love every person, even those who slay them. They will even love every tree, rock, building, street—everything! They will have the reality of paradise within their hearts, and that reality will be greater than anything in the physical realm. This love will result in the conversion of multitudes. As fear is the greatest power of the evil one, love is the greatest power of heaven, and when they collide in their last and ultimate battle, love will win.

This is the preparation for the saints for the last battle—to grow in love, faith and obedience. This will bring power over all of the powers of darkness that will be released in the last days, which will be rooted in hatred, fear and lawlessness.

Because lawlessness will be prevailing in the world during this time, even the world's armies will be little more than mobs controlled by fear and intimidation. When the grip of fear is relaxed to any degree, such as when there is the death of a powerful leader, these armies will quickly disintegrate into chaos. However, the army of the Lord will display a level of unity, discipline and coordination of efforts that will be unprecedented in the history of civilization, and will continue advancing without faltering when her visible leaders are lost.

In the last days the church will shine like a great lighthouse, pointing the way to the safety of the harbor. The darker it becomes the more power that she will be given to shine through it. The raging storms will drive even more sojourners to her light and to her prepared haven.

The Army Is A Bride

In the last days the church will become the most beautiful bride. Heaven and earth will marvel at her glory and purity. The reproach of centuries of unfaithfulness with the spirit of the world will be wiped away by the Spirit of holiness. This holiness will not be a form of legalism—it will be the passionate devotion of the bride to her Betrothed—Jesus. The church will purify herself because of love, not law.

In the last days the church will be a family. She will reveal to the world the true meaning of family. In her house there will be places for sons and daughters, fathers and mothers, grandfathers and grandmothers, aunts and uncles, and cousins from every tribe and nation on the face of the earth. The church in the last days will give the world a revelation of FAMILY that will begin to heal the wounds that originated when the first two brothers could not live together peacefully.

In the last days the church will be a great hospital with the power to heal every kind of wound and disease. She will have a cure for every new plague. When despair comes in like a flood, the joy of the Lord will be her medicine, and the world will beat a path to her door to partake of it.

How will the church be all of these things? She will be united to the Lord, take His name, and manifest Him to the world. He is all of this and more, and the church is about to become the witness of His nature that she has been called to be. He is the Lord of hosts (armies); He is the Bridegroom; He is our Father; He is our Healer, and the world is going to know it. There will be a witness through the church of who our God is before the end can come.

The Safe Harbor

As the testimony of Scripture reveals that in the last days the earth will suffer its greatest assaults from wars, earthquakes, famines and plagues, the church will provide a haven from each. As wars increase the church will reveal the peace of God. As earthquakes shake the foundations of the earth, the church will be a testimony that there is a foundation that cannot be shaken, and when we build our lives upon it the whole earth can fall apart but we will not be moved. As famines grip the earth the church will reveal that there is a supernatural provision for the saints, and they will never be found begging for bread. When plagues traverse whole continents, the church will come forth with the power to heal any disease, making known the haven in Christ where no plague can come near.

We are now in the time when everything that can be shaken is being shaken—and the shaking is obviously intensifying. So let us not be lulled into a false tranquility based on world conditions if it seems that we are entering a period of stability—the Lord has sent His angels to hold back the winds of the earth for a period so that we can be sealed as His bondservants. This time of peace is for our preparation—let us use it wisely, not wasting a single day.

See to it that you do not refuse Him who is speaking. For if those did not escape when they refused him who warned them on earth, much

less shall we escape who turn away from Him who warns from heaven.

And His voice shook the earth then, but now He has promised, saying, "Yet once more I will shake not only the earth, but also the heaven."

And this expression, "Yet once more," denotes the removing of those things which can be shaken, as of created things, in order that those things which cannot be shaken may remain.

Therefore, since we receive a kingdom which cannot be shaken, let us show gratitude, by which we may offer to God an acceptable service with reverence and awe;

for our God is a consuming fire (Hebrews 12:25-29).

Chapter Nine

Avoiding Shipwreck

The shipwreck suffered by Paul in Acts 27 highlights important principles which, if understood and applied, can save every believer a considerable amount of trouble in this life.

As with most revelations in the Word, these can be applied on several levels: they relate to us as individuals, they relate to our congregations, to the corporate body of Christ, even to nations. They apply to ministries, businesses and families. In a general sense they can be applied to almost any situation.

There were four main factors which led the crew of Paul's ship to place themselves in danger of destruction.

They Were Dissatisfied With Their Circumstances

The crew of Paul's ship did not feel that the port they were in "was adequate for spending the winter" (verse 12). This tendency to be guided by dissatisfaction with circumstances, or people, rather than by the Holy Spirit is the cause of many spiritual shipwrecks. Our spiritual walk is supposed to take us from "glory to glory," not from defeat to defeat. When we are dissatisfied we should be more inclined *not* to leave a situation, but to wait instead for the glory of victory.

The one message that the Lord gave to each of the seven churches in Revelation was that they were to be "overcomers." To be an overcomer means that we must refuse to be overcome by circumstances and opposition. The tendency to be led by circumstances, or to allow the force of opposition to dictate our course, has led to many grievous mistakes.

They Were Impatient

It is clear that the crew of Paul's ship was in a hurry to get to Rome. *Impatience combined with dissatisfaction is a deadly combination.* The Scriptures are full of exhortations to wait upon God. I do not know of a single one that encourages us to hurry up or we will miss Him!

Spiritual atrophy and lukewarmness are serious problems in the church. Some believers do need to get moving because they are being left behind. Even so, if we start moving just to be moving we will still almost certainly end up in the wrong place. We must be following the Lamb, not impatience. As Israel learned in the wilderness, there are times when the Lord's cloud will move and times when we will be called upon just to camp where we are. If the Lord stops and we keep moving, regardless of how great our zeal for Him is, we will have missed Him. We will be out of His will and may very well have difficulty finding Him again.

The Scriptures have many more exhortations to wait upon the Lord because those who really love Him and want to serve Him are more inclined to run ahead than to be too slow to move. We must remember that impatience is *not* a fruit of the spirit.

They Failed To Heed
The Word Of The Lord

Paul had received a clear word of warning, **"But the centurion was more persuaded by the pilot and the captain of the ship, than by what was being said by Paul" (verse 11).** This is often the result of our being impatient and dissatisfied. Those who are so inclined will usually disregard the word of the Lord when it comes, and will keep looking until they find someone whose opinion confirms what they want to do. This is a most dangerous practice, and it is a primary reason for many of the defeats and shipwrecks we leave in our own wake.

They Looked To Circumstances
To Give Them Guidance

"When a moderate south wind came up, supposing that they had gained their purpose, they weighed anchor and began sailing" (Verse 13). The teaching that circumstances will always line up with the guidance from the Lord is another erroneous assumption to which many Christians adhere. This too cannot be substantiated by the Scriptures.

The biblical testimony is that obedience to many, if not most, of the directive words of the Lord will require an *overcoming* of circumstances. There are some examples where circumstances would become favorable through compliance with the directive, and there are even a few where the Lord miraculously intervened to make them favorable. However, these are an exception to the pattern and are by no means substantial enough to constitute general principles. We are to follow the Lamb, not circumstances. "For all who are being led by the Spirit of God, these are sons of God" (Romans 8:14). We are to be led by the Spirit of God from within, not by external circumstances.

These are four negative factors that put the crew of Paul's ship in jeopardy of shipwreck. I have observed these same factors operating in the lives of believers and churches which has led to the same disastrous conclusion. Those who do not learn these lessons inevitably live tragic lives of repetitious defeat. Simply recognizing these factors can help break the cycle in our lives.

The Proper Use Of Prophecy

There are many widespread misconceptions about directive prophecy and spiritual guidance which have also led to many problems. One such teaching concerning personal and directive prophecy states that these should *only* represent confirmation to the believer. This principle seems wise and logical but cannot be supported biblically. In fact, the biblical record is contrary to this teaching and holding to this fallacy will often create a potential for calamity.

First, we must understand; there are times when prophecies do come as needed confirmation. However, it is the teaching that this is *always* the case that is spurious. This teaching dangerously assumes that the Lord will always speak to us two or more times before we are required to hear Him. The Lord is not like the parent who has allowed his children to get so out of control that they do not hear directives until they have been given several times, and then it's usually by raising their voices! The Lord expects us to hear His voice even when it is a "still small voice," and even when it comes in the midst of earthquakes, wind and fire.

The overall testimony of Scripture is that the Lord usually only speaks one time, and only rarely confirms it. Paul's warning of impending danger to their ship was apparently the only one they were given, and it obviously did not come as a confirmation to the centurion. The centurion's determination to seek other counsel when he did not like the word of the Lord led him to a shipwreck, just as it has a number of other biblical characters as it continues to do for numerous present day believers.

The biblical testimony is that *usually,* when directive words of prophecy are given, they are in direct conflict with the leading or direction of the person to whom they are given. Sometimes the true words of the Lord stood alone, in contrast to that of all other witnesses, counselors and even "prophets," opposing the direction the leaders were inclined to go. In almost every case the leader who did not heed the *one* word paid a terrible price for rejecting it. There are a few cases when confirmation of the word was sought, such as with Gideon, but this is actually the exception to the rule rather than the standard.

King Josiah was one of the most righteous, and spiritually sensitive kings in the history of Judah. By the Lord's own testimony he removed more evil from the land than even his forefather David had, and he led the greatest revival in the history of the nation. Even so, when Neco the king of Egypt intended to pass through his land on his way to the Euphrates, the Lord warned Josiah, *through Neco* (his enemy no less) not to make war with him. However, Josiah would not be dissuaded, **"nor did he listen to the words of Neco *from the mouth of God"* (II Chronicles 35:22).** The result of this righteous king not discerning the voice of the Lord, spoken just once and through a most unlikely source, was that he perished in the ensuing battle.

Again, there are some examples in both the New and Old Testaments of the Lord giving confirmation to His prophetic words, but these are the exception to the rule. When we make such broad generalizations with our principles we must be sure that they comply with the biblical testimony rather than accepting them because they sound reasonable.

Some argue that personal prophecy should always come as confirmation based on the Scripture that **"Every fact is to be confirmed by the testimony of two or three witnesses" (II Corinthians 13:1 & Deuteronomy 17:6).** However, Paul's reference here is not about prophecy. He is quoting the Old Testament verse concerning receiving a legal witness against another. In neither reference is prophecy or directive guidance the subject of this commandment. This misconception is simply the result of faulty hermeneutics.

The True Test Of Guidance

Many of the popular "principles" that are taught concerning how to judge prophecy seem to be an attempt to avoid the most important factor in distinguishing true words from false—*knowing the Lord's voice*. The issue to validating prophetic words is not how many we receive, but rather the clarity and anointing on the words themselves. If we are leaders in the body of Christ, which every believer is called to be to some degree, our first responsibility is to be able to hear the directives of our Leader—Jesus. The Lord's sheep know His voice. Even the most logical principles cannot be substituted for this one essential.

The way that sheep come to know their shepherd's voice is by being with him. In this same way we will come to know the voice of our Shepherd. The more time we have spent with Him, the better we will know His voice. There is no substitute for this.

Discernment Comes From Knowing The Real

I was once told of a man who worked for the Treasury Department whose sole job was to handle money. He became so familiar with the feel of real currency that he would know instantly when he was handed a counterfeit bill. In this same way we must become so familiar with the true word, that if any other person or spirit speaks to us, we will know instantly that it is not the Lord.

Had this man at the Treasury Department spent his time handling counterfeit money he would probably never have been able to recognize true currency. The same is true spiritually. Few who devote themselves to studying cults or deviant doctrines are able to distinguish the true word of the Lord, and usually their hearts are ultimately darkened by the very evil they seek to expose. We will be changed into that which we are beholding (II Corinthians 3:18). There is an implied warning in the Lord's message to the church in Thyatira about **"knowing the deep things of Satan" (Revelation 2:24).** The more we focus on what is wrong, or the practices of the evil one, the more we, ourselves, will be changed into the nature of what we are seeing. That is why Paul exhorts us to **"Prove all things [which implies to test them],** *hold fast that which is good"* **[not that which is bad]. (I Thessalonians 5:21 KJV).**

I once read an amazing story about the ability of sheep to distinguish their shepherd's voice. The author of this story was sitting on a hill overlooking a watering hole when he observed three different, large flocks of sheep being led to it simultaneously. He perceived an impending, serious problem for the shepherds—that their flocks would get so mixed that they would never be able to separate them again! Amazingly, the shepherds seemed unconcerned as they stood talking to each other and the flocks intermingled. Then, after the sheep had all been watered, each shepherd took a different path and began singing as he walked. There was a great convulsion in the huge mixed flock; then little streams of sheep began to follow behind each shepherd as he walked and sang. Soon they had all separated into their individual flocks behind their own shepherds. Even when all of the shepherds were singing at the same time, those sheep knew their own master's voice and were able to distinguish it.

This is a wonderful illustration of how we, too, must know our Shepherd's voice. Knowing the voice of the Lord is not dependent upon how many times He speaks, or even how He speaks; it is dependent upon knowing *Who* is speaking. We can, and must be able to distinguish His voice from all of the others that are clamoring for our attention. There is no shortcut or substitute for simply being with Him and communicating with Him.

Instant Obedience

If we teach our children that they do not really have to obey us until we have repeated ourselves several times and then raised our voices, they will not respond to us until we go through that process. The children who are taught by their parents to obey the first time will hear and respond with the first command. It is a terrible, and often costly, presumption when we refuse to hear and respond to the Lord the first time He speaks to us, regardless of whether it is what we want to do or not. God is not like weak, inconsistent parents.

There are numerous men and women of God who suffer shipwreck after shipwreck in their lives because they are like the centurion on Paul's ship. When they hear the word of the Lord, it is not what they want to hear. Then it is convenient to use such excuses as not having any confirmation for the word, so they seek the opinions of others until they find one they like. This will set them up to follow circumstances which lead to shipwreck.

Grace For The Willing

In John 7:17 the Lord states, **"If any man is willing to do His will, he shall know of the teaching, whether it is of God, or whether I speak from Myself."** We must understand the Lord is a strict, but loving Father. What good parent would be upset with a child that really wanted to obey, but had a hearing problem and sometimes misunderstood directives? The Lord is full of grace and mercy for the willing, obedient heart.

There is also grace for the immature. The Lord specified that His *sheep* knew His voice, not His lambs. Lambs are expected to follow the more mature until their own senses have been trained through experience. Many biblical characters, who died or suffered loss for failure to heed the word of the Lord, were holding positions of leadership that required the highest standards of discernment and obedience. These standards cannot be compromised. The greater the authority and influence, the higher the standards which are required.

Many are bound by such a fear that they will miss the Lord and His directives that they are easily subjected to false leadings by the enemy or by the confusion in their own hearts. The Lord does not lead through fear; He leads us by faith. **"The wisdom (or leading) from above is first pure, then peaceable, gentle, reasonable, full of mercy and good fruits, unwavering, without hypocrisy.** *And the seed whose fruit is righteousness is sown in peace by those who make peace"* (James 3:17-18).

The Lord knows our weaknesses and He is full of grace and mercy. He is not busy looking for reasons to judge us; He is always seeking ways to show us mercy and grace. He does not pressure us with fears that we will miss Him; the wisdom that He gives comes with His peace.

When I am not sure if I am hearing from the Lord *I ask Him to speak to me again,* especially when it has to do with a major decision, or if it is contrary to what I believe is the right course of action. But I do not do this because I am demanding a right; I go to the throne of grace seeking grace to help me in my need—because I am still so dull of hearing. However, I do not always expect Him to do this because I understand that it is not biblical to expect it. There is a point at which He simply expects us to obey without further discussion.

It is my hope to mature to the place where, like Elijah in the cave, I will always be sensitive to hear His voice regardless of the circumstances, confusion or distractions. That is maturity. That is why the Lord said that His *sheep* know His voice.

Part II

How To Get Out Of The Storm

There was a reason why the Lord wanted to restrain Paul's ship from leaving the port. Even though it did not seem adequate for the winter, the Lord knew about the storm that was coming. We often presume that God will not allow us to get into a storm, which is why many get into unnecessary troubles.

Of course, it would have been an easy thing for the Lord to calm the storm that came upon Paul's ship. However, He is usually far more interested in changing the attitudes of our hearts which keep getting us into such storms. Adam and Eve's obvious dissatisfaction with their circumstances was what started all of our problems in the first place. This is still at the root of all of our problems, and we will never get back to the peace and harmony that was known in the Garden until it is rooted out of us.

The Scriptures warn us that, as we come to the end of this age, we will be entering into the greatest time of troubles that the world has ever known. Many Christians believe that they will escape these troubles through the rapture. Even if this is the case, what is described as just "the beginning of birth pangs" is catastrophic in itself. It is therefore imperative that we know how to deal with troubles even if we are going to escape that which is called "the great tribulation." If we learn to handle them properly, every difficulty we experience will lead us closer to the Lord.

The storms we get ourselves into will ultimately help to work contentment into our lives; it is amazing how good that "inadequate" port will look from the midst of the storm! The issue is—how many storms will be required for us to learn contentment in whatever state the Lord has us? If we would learn to be patient in the Lord, listen to Him and follow Him only, to calm the voice of our personal ambition, and not to be deceived by favorable circumstances, only the Lord Himself knows how much grief we would save ourselves and His people during the span of our lifetime.

There Is A Way Out

What should we do if we are already in the midst of a storm? Even if we got into our present mess because of our dissatisfaction, impatience or not heeding the Lord's warnings, *we can still get out of the storm without losing everything.* Even if you have made all of the mistakes listed above, do not panic; there is still a way out of your storm.

Remarkably, the actions that the crew of Paul's ship took in the storm are consistently what should *not* be done to successfully navigate through a storm. These same actions reflect the pattern that most people follow when reacting to problems. Human reasoning is often contrary to the ways of the Lord, but under pressure that reasoning can often become irrational. We must understand this reasoning if we are to escape its folly. The following are principles that can help us to navigate the storms of life, but often they are contrary to what we may feel like doing.

Principle #1. We must prepare for the storms *before* we get into them.

If we are going to be prepared to get through the storms, we must understand that they are inevitable. There are storms that we must go through even when we are on course and moving in the will of the Lord. When the Lord compared the house (life) that had been built upon the rock, which was built by both hearing *and* heeding the word of the Lord, a storm came upon it too. Paul said, **"Through many tribulations we must enter the kingdom of God"** (Acts 14:22).

A recent phenomenon to come out of the Western church has been the subtle concept that it is not the will of God for Christians to have problems. This is contrary to the biblical testimony which speaks of the faith to have victory over problems, not to escape from them. It is true that we do not want to go through storms that are not necessary, which are caused by our own self-will. Even so, we must be prepared to navigate through the storms that we are destined to go through, as well as the ones that we get ourselves into—the Lord wants to get us out of those, too!

As a professional pilot I had to learn a lot about weather for the specific purpose of avoiding storms. Even "all weather" fighters do all that they can to avoid thunderstorms. Not only can the lightning be dangerous, but the most violent turbulence on earth can be found in a thunderhead. There can be an updraft rising at six thousand feet per minute right next to a down draft of six thousand feet per minute—going from one to the other can tear the wings off of your plane. But even if you get into a thunderhead, you will probably come out of it *if* you follow the proper procedures. Remarkably, these procedures parallel the biblical counsel of navigating the storms of life.

When I decided to become a pilot, I was determined to be the best pilot that I could possibly become. I requested the toughest instructors. Later, after I had become an instructor, I took a job flying with a man who was considered one of the world's best pilots. He seemed to take great pleasure at exposing my flaws and mistakes. He would put as much pressure on me as he possibly could on each flight—even the smallest mistake would draw either ridicule or rage. There would be days when I would come home from the airport never wanting to even see another airplane. Later in my career, when I got into storms or faced other emergencies, I was very thankful for all of the pressure this man put me under.

Once I got into a storm that exceeded any I had ever experienced. Not only was I nearly blinded by lightning which struck my plane, but the turbulence was so bad that for minutes at a time I could not read my instruments to know whether I was right side up or upside down. When my arms became so weary from fighting the controls that I did not think that I could go on, I cried out to God for a miracle to get me out of the storm. His reply was quick but firm: *"Your training was My grace to get you through."*

I am thankful for the miracles when we get them, but often we do not need a miracle as much as we need endurance. The writer of Hebrews explained, **"But remember the former days, when, after being enlightened, you endured a great conflict of sufferings... For you have need of endurance, so that when you have done the will of God, you may receive what was promised" (Hebrews 10:32,36).** Trials are for the purpose of working God's grace into our lives. One of the most important lessons we can learn to get us through our lives on course is *to not waste a good trial,* but to make the most of every opportunity. The lessons we learn from them may someday save our spiritual lives.

Consider some of the following promises from the Bible. These are probably not the ones that we have tacked onto our refrigerators so that we can claim them everyday, but are nevertheless the Word of God.

"For to you it has been granted for Christ's sake, not only to believe in Him, *but also to suffer for His sake***, experiencing the same conflict which you saw in me, and now hear to be in me" (Philippians 1:29-30).**

What was this suffering Paul was experiencing? He tells us in II Corinthians 4:8-11:

We are afflicted in every way, but not crushed; perplexed, but not despairing; persecuted, but not forsaken; struck down, but not destroyed;

always carrying about in the body the dying of Jesus, *[in order] that* the life of Jesus also may be manifested in our body.

For we who live are constantly being delivered over to death for Jesus's sake, that the life of Jesus also may be manifested in our mortal flesh.

Paul is saying here that *death is the path of life* in Christ. The Lord Jesus said the same thing in other words when He stated what was required of those who would follow Him:

If *anyone* [not just preachers or ministers, but <u>anyone</u>] wishes to come after Me, *let him deny himself, and take up his cross,* and follow Me.

For whoever wishes to save his life shall lose it; but whoever loses his life for My sake shall find it (Matthew 16:24-25).

Paul further encourages us:

And indeed, all who desire to live godly in Christ Jesus *will* be persecuted (II Timothy 3:12).

… [you are] in no way alarmed by your opponents—which is a sign of destruction for them, but of salvation for you, and that too, from God (Philippians 1:28).

Have you ever considered that the opposition coming against you is "a sign of your salvation"? Paul's encouragement to the Corinthians continued:

For momentary, light affliction is producing for us an eternal weight of glory far beyond all comparison,

while we look not at the things which are seen, but at the things which are not seen; for the things which are seen are temporal, but the things which are not seen are eternal (II Corinthians 4:17-18).

When the eyes of our hearts are opened to see the things which are eternal, we really are able to:

Consider it all joy, my brethren, when you encounter various trials, knowing that the testing of your faith produces endurance.

And let endurance have its perfect result, that you may be perfect and complete, lacking in nothing (James 1:2-4).

Principle #2. You must stay calm in the midst of the storm.

Panic almost certainly kills more pilots than the actual storms. Panic destroys our judgment and our ability to function properly. When the Lord Jesus and His disciples got into a storm, He confronted it with *"Peace! Be still."* Our first priority must be to focus on the peace of the Lord, not the tension generated by the storm. Your own panic in the midst of a storm can be far more deadly than the storm itself.

Principle #3. You must keep your wings level.

Every flight manual recommends this for turbulence penetration. Keeping your wings level speaks of maintaining *balance* when every natural tendency is to begin reacting and therefore overreacting to the storm. Once a pilot starts overreacting to turbulence, he is close to losing control of the aircraft.

Also, the stress on the aircraft just from the turbulence can be close to the limits of what it can take. If we start overreacting on the controls we are adding to that stress. This is what happens to many churches, ministries, movements and individuals who drift into the extremes—they get into a storm and then start overreacting. This presses them beyond the limits of what the people can bear, and the ship starts breaking up.

Principle #4. You must hold your course.

The quickest way out of a storm is to go *straight* through it. Flight manuals, instructors and experienced pilots will all tell you *not to turn around* when you get into a storm. The largest thunderheads are usually only a few miles wide. When you try to turn around in the storm, you will stay in it longer than if you just flew straight.

The crew of Paul's ship let themselves be driven by the storm—*they let the storm dictate the course*. Just as this was the beginning of the end of Paul's ship, it is usually the beginning of the end of ours. The way out of the storm is not by submitting to it but by overcoming it. Great pressure will come upon us during the storm to make changes or try new courses to get out of the storm—resist them! **"Make straight paths for your feet"** (Hebrews 12:13). *Hold your course!*

Principle #5. Do not abandon your cargo while in the storm.

The next reaction of the crew of Paul's ship was to jettison the cargo. This is a common reaction of people who get into problems; we begin to abandon the teachings, relationships, and often even the church that the Lord has given us to help us through such problems. Remember that the cargo is usually the purpose for the journey. Cargo includes the things we are to carry to our destination. We must not easily abandon them when we get into a storm.

Most of us do have a great deal of excess baggage that we could stand to get rid of, but the time to start throwing things out is not while we're in the storm. Our judgment will not be as good in the pressure of trials, and we will almost certainly throw out many things that we should have retained. The worst mistakes I have made as a Christian were caused by my tendency to get rid of my "excess baggage" while in the midst of a storm. In the storm, hold your course, *and hold on to what God has given you.*

Principle #6. Do not submit to the storm—submit to God.

The next thing the crew of Paul's ship did was to throw out the ship's tackle. That Paul stated "with our own hands" indicates that he was amazed they could do such a thing. With the ship's tackle gone, they had no hope of steering the ship again. They had totally abandoned themselves to the storm. The Lord wants us to live in submission to His will, but this is not the same as submission to circumstances. When the Lord gives us a course, we should steer. If we are controlled by circumstances, we will be blown about by every wind and will end up almost certainly far from the course He has given us.

When I first started flying I was amazed when I looked down at the course of rivers. I knew that rivers meandered, but I never knew that they twisted and turned to the degree that they do. Because they twist and bend so much, they usually have to go many times the distance to get from point to point than they would if they just flowed in a straight line. Why do rivers twist and turn so much? Because water always takes the path of least resistance. Likewise, people who are prone to always take the path of least resistance will be continually turning and twisting in their lives, having to travel many times the distance and expending many times the effort to get to their destinations. Again, *the Lord commanded us to* **"strengthen the hands that are weak and the knees that are feeble, and *make straight paths for your feet*" (Hebrews 12:12-13).** He has not called us to submit to resistance; He has called us to overcome it.

Principle #7. Never lose your hope.

The crew of Paul's ship abandoned all hope and stopped eating. Even if we have made many mistakes and put ourselves into such difficult circumstances, we must never give up hope, and we must not stop eating. As Paul had previously written to the Romans (he was traveling to Rome on this ship):

… we also exult in our tribulations, knowing that tribulation brings about perseverance;

and perseverance, proven character; and proven character, *hope; and hope does not disappoint* **(Romans 5:3-5)**

That is a sure promise from God—our hope will not disappoint us. Hebrews 6:18-19 states: "**[Because] it is impossible for God to lie, we may have strong encouragement, we who have fled for refuge in laying hold of the** *hope* **set before us.** *This hope we have as an anchor for the soul*, **a hope both sure and steadfast and one which enters within the veil.**"

Hope is the anchor our soul needs in the midst of storms and rough seas. It is actually hope that enables us to enter into the presence of the Lord ("within the veil"). Despair and depression are our greatest enemies during periods of trial and conflict. When the first generation of the children of Israel who came out of Egypt gave themselves to depression, it led to their grumbling and complaining, which led to their destruction and failure to enter the promised land. It will do the same for us.

Never abandon your hope. Never give yourself to complaining.

Also like the crew of Paul's ship, we often begin to neglect eating when we get in such intense circumstances. It is amazing how we tend to neglect our daily feeding on the Word of God when we need it the most. Neglecting this is probably the main reason why we lose our hope and faith while in the midst of the trials.

When we make the same mistakes that the crew of Paul's ship did, we will get into unnecessary storms. If we continue to make those same mistakes in the midst of the storm, we will suffer loss. Even so, the great encouragement of the whole story of Acts 27 is found in the results of their adventure. Even though they lost the ship, its "fragments" made life preservers so that *1) not a soul was lost, 2) they were provided with a safe haven for spending the rest of the winter and, 3) they were provided with another ship in order to finish their journey.*

Summary

When we begin to combine *dissatisfaction* with *impatience* we have a deadly combination. Add to them the *failure to heed the word of the Lord* and we are primed for the knockout punch of being deceived by *favorable circumstances,* never suspecting the terrible storm that follows right behind them.

How many individuals, dissatisfied with their homes, cars or other "needs" (often goaded by commercial advertising), when they receive a raise, promotion or indications that one is coming, succumb to impatience and go into debt? Then the storm comes and they suffer a layoff, or other cutback, or they just do not get the raise. Many stay on the thin edge of disaster financially, or actually suffer shipwreck because of this pattern.

How many churches or ministries, being dissatisfied with their present buildings or meeting place, become convinced that a new building would cause them to grow? The Lord may have in fact given them a vision of growth but they just cannot wait for the proper timing of the Lord. So they strive for their new facilities to the degree that they lose touch with the Lord and His anointing. Then they end up with twice the building and half the people they already had, because those people were coming for the Lord, not a building. The Lord will bless faith but He will not bless presumption, or impatience. If we are moved by dissatisfaction or impatience we are sailing in dangerous seas.

There are many believers who are "church hoppers." They never become fruitful members of the body of Christ because they bail out any time the "port starts looking inadequate." How many never become established, fruitful members of the body of Christ because they are impatient for the perfect church that just is not found on this earth? These almost all go on to become the ones Jude called **"clouds without water, carried along by winds; trees without fruit, doubly dead,...** *for whom the black darkness has been reserved forever"* (Jude 12-13).

Idealism is an enemy of the truth! Some of the books projecting the ideal, perfect church have done more to put stumbling blocks in the path of the church becoming mature and effective than hoards of false doctrines. We need to have a vision of maturity and the Lord's standards and purposes for His church, but idealism is from within the human heart; it is from the "good" side of the Tree Of Knowledge of Good and Evil. The good side of that tree is just as deadly as the evil side; they both have the same root. Those who project the "ideal church" in a spirit of criticism toward those that do not meet up to their standards can put themselves in a worse jeopardy than those who are falling short of the Lord's standards.

Those who are led by dissatisfaction and impatience usually become the very ones about which Jude warned the church—the **"grumblers, finding fault, following after their own lusts; they speak arrogantly, flattering people for the sake of gaining an advantage**... **these are the ones who cause divisions" (Jude 16,19).** Those who are led by dissatisfaction and impatience usually become the church hoppers who can be found behind many church divisions, spreading their poison of discontent everywhere they go. The Lord Himself said that it would be better for us not to have been born than to cause even one of His little ones to stumble; this is the very last type of person we ever want to become!

We may be "saved," born again, baptized in the Holy Spirit, read our Bibles and pray more than anyone else, but the Lord Jesus Himself warned that it would be better for us to have never been born than to cause even one of

His little ones to stumble. These "grumblers and fault finders" often spend their lives causing others to stumble and will be in serious trouble when they stand before the Him on that day. Those who are led by impatience and dissatisfaction will become bitter souls, inevitably blaming everyone but themselves for their failures, and their roots of bitterness will almost always go on to defile many others.

There will be times when the "ports" we're in will not look adequate to us—and they will have inadequacies! However, it is when we are inadequate that God's grace makes up the difference, where we begin to see His miraculous provision. It is usually just before He moves that impatience will exert its greatest pressure, even a "spiritual" impatience to fulfill what we know is the calling of God. If we allow impatience to guide us it will result in defeat. Often that defeat comes just before the breakthrough that God had planned.

The Lord is very faithful to speak to us at that time, but we are often too distracted by the agitation of our souls to hear Him. We must learn not to let impatience or dissatisfaction become our guides—they will usually lead us into a worse situation than we were in before. We must learn to **"Let the peace of Christ rule in your hearts"** (Colossians 3:15). For **"The wisdom from above is first pure, then peaceable, gentle, reasonable, full of mercy and good fruits, unwavering, without hypocrisy. And** *the seed whose fruit is righteousness is sown in peace by those who make peace"* **(James 3:17-18).**

RAGP 12/03

Only when we have learned to be led by the Spirit (whose fruit is love, joy, peace, patience, kindness, goodness, faithfulness, gentleness and self-control, which are exactly contrary to dissatisfaction and impatience) will we go from "glory to glory" instead of from defeat to defeat.

I have watched individuals, families, ministries, churches, Christian communities and businesses suffer shipwreck because of these same factors. In every case the ship would run aground and begin to break up until there were just fragments left. Yet, the Lord would always be faithful to then provide another ship. *If* we will abide in His grace, we will still go through storms, but we will never suffer shipwreck. However, if we make the mistake of not abiding in His grace so that we do suffer shipwreck, there is still mercy that is always ready to restore us and give us another chance. Even so, isn't it time that we quit wrecking the ships that He gives us?

Let us be content with the "port" the Lord has us in, and stay there until He directs us to leave. Let us not be led by dissatisfaction and impatience, but let us instead abide in contentment in whatever circumstances *He* has us in. It will take both **"faith *and* patience to inherit the promises" (Hebrews 6:12).** We must not be so easily fooled by the first breeze that's blowing the way we want to go, when we've been told to wait. I have never been in a "shipwreck," nor have I ever observed one, which was not caused by impatience. We may blame our problems on the devil but I do not think that he deserves as much credit as we have given him. When we learn to **"let the peace of God rule in our hearts"** (Colossians 3:15), we will have smooth sailing.

Chapter Ten

Building On A Sure Foundation

In recent revivals a high percentage of those who committed themselves to the Lord were lost again to the world. This happened chiefly because the church was not prepared to care for the new believers. The Lord is giving His church a strategy so that this will not happen again. We must accept this mandate as both the highest honor and highest responsibility with which we could ever be entrusted. These are the children of the King of kings whom He is trusting us to spiritually feed and protect.

We must have spiritual nets that are strong enough to hold the great ingathering that is coming. To do this the church in general must raise her vision, strategy and mutual co-operation to a new level. Those who gather must be properly linked to those who can teach and help lay a proper foundation in a new believer's life. As one friend of mine put it: "Those who catch the fish must learn to give them to those who will clean them."

If those who are equipped and anointed to catch the fish are then obliged to stop and clean them, the whole process will slow down. This has caused the end of some revivals. Just as the apostles and other ministries in the first century learned to work in harmony, with one planting and another coming along to water the seeds that were planted, both knowing that only God could cause

177

the increase, we must lay aside our self-interests and do the same.

True Conversion

In the first century the only ones who were counted as converts were those who were "added to the church." The great commission was not to go out and make converts, but to make disciples. In our evangelical zeal to save people from damnation we may sometimes be guilty of sealing their damnation with a salvation message that has only inoculated them against the true salvation. Is a man truly converted who does not go on to be a living, functioning member of the body of Christ? According to the biblical testimony we would have to doubt it.

Philip is the only example that we have in Scripture of a pure evangelist. When he had stirred the city of Samaria with the gospel, apostles were then dispatched to follow up his work, ensuring that the new believers were sealed with the Holy Spirit. When the Lord sent out His disciples in Luke 10, He sent them only to places "… **where He Himself was going to come" (verse 1).** In other words, He only sent His ministries to where He was going to follow up their work.

Because there is a premium on the laborers for the harvest, and all of our time and effort is precious, we must be discerning not to waste our efforts going anywhere we are not sure that the Lord is going to follow up the work. The Lord does not just want us to bear fruit, but to bear fruit that remains. As laborers we must think strategically, and we must think as teams.

Many of the large evangelistic crusades today are planned for months, or even years. Churches are mobilized, intercessory teams are established, and an army of counselors are trained in the targeted city or region. Even so, some of the great evangelists of our time have lamented that only about five percent of those who make a "decision" for Christ actually continue more than a couple of weeks in the faith. Certainly we should be very thankful for this five percent! For some of these ministries this has still added up to multitudes of true conversions that have born lasting fruit. Even so, neither can we be satisfied with this low percentage of fruit that remains.

This low retention rate of people who make a commitment to the Lord relates to both the poor quality of the decision and the ineffectiveness of the nets. The quality of a decision may or may not have anything to do with the evangelist. The Lord Jesus was obviously the ultimate evangelist, yet on several occasions most of those who followed Him departed. As He explained, this particular work of the kingdom is like casting a dragnet. Anyone who has fished with a dragnet learns quickly that only a small portion of the catch can be kept.

It is also true that *commitment* has become an increasingly diluted virtue in modern times. Both initiative and resolve are required for advancement, spiritual or otherwise, and these are directly related to a person's willingness to take responsibility for his own actions. Blame-shifting was the immediate result of the fall (Adam blamed the woman and the woman blamed the serpent), and those who blame others, or their circumstances, for failure, are abiding in their sins.

The enemy has been very successful in dulling the vision and potential of modern man to embrace the cross by inculcating a "victim mentality." True repentance is impossible until we admit that *we* have sinned and need forgiveness. In an attempt to reach modern man, many have adjusted their gospel to appeal to man's needs, which has profoundly diluted the gospel and its power to save men from this thick and deceptive veil.

Saved From What?

There is a widespread mentality in the church today that men will not come to the Lord until they are in desperate circumstances. Circumstances can be used to get someone's attention, but they are by no means required, or even important. The only thing that a person needs to come to repentance is the conviction of sin by the Holy Spirit. The reason for this mentality that desperate circumstances are required to bring one to Christ is because our modern gospel has been changed to a message that He came to save us from our troubles instead of from our sins.

In John 6 we see that when Jesus walked on the earth many followed Him for different reasons. Some did so because they saw the miracles; others followed because He fed them with the loaves and fishes. Discerning this

He challenged the multitude by declaring that, if they did not eat His flesh and drink His blood, they had no part in Him. Because of this "hard saying" we read that **"Many therefore of His disciples, when they heard this said, 'This is a difficult statement; who can listen to it?'… As a result of this many of His disciples withdrew, and were not walking with Him any more" (verses 60,66).** By preaching the power of God and the provision of God we can get multitudes to follow Jesus, but they will not partake of Him.

When men are compelled to follow Jesus because He will take care of their problems, then, when their problems continue, or other ones arise, they will cease to believe the message they were given—and they should! It was a lie. **"Through many tribulations we must enter the kingdom of God" (Acts 14:22).** We are not delivered *from* tribulations, we are delivered *through* them.

However, when a person comes to Jesus because he is convicted of sin, he embraces the cross. The greater the depth of conviction, the greater the grip that he will have on it. When we are convicted of how continuously evil we are, we will pick up the cross everyday and carry it with us everywhere. When such are then challenged to see if they too will depart from Him, they will respond as Peter did: **"Lord, to whom shall we go? You have the words of eternal life…" (John 6:68).** These are not so captivated by the temporary provisions, but by the eternal provision. Then the provision and the power of God will be appreciated, but kept in their proper place.

The Cost Of Discipleship

The Lord Jesus made it hard to join and easy to leave. He wanted those who joined to be committed unto death. In fact, He often required those who followed Him to leave everything that they had behind. He then said and did things that appeared to purposely sift out those who might not have been totally committed, or who were committed for the wrong reasons. Everything about the Lord, and His apostles, seemed designed to purposely repel those who might come to Him for any other reason than a heart conviction that He was the Way, the Truth, and the Life which was worth dying for.

Somehow modern evangelism seems to have reversed this wisdom of the gospel—we make it as easy as we can for men to join, and then as hard as we can for them to leave. This is a foundational issue, and it affects the quality of the foundation of what we are building. Much of what is now being promulgated as the gospel may be actually dooming men to damnation because it compels them to feel safe though their condition, in fact, has them in terrible spiritual jeopardy.

Make The Wedding Grand

I have now been married for seventeen years, and I still think that one of our most difficult times was preparing for the wedding. It was then that I came to understand that any relationship that can survive preparation for a large wedding should easily be able to endure anything else that comes against it. However, the wedding day itself was one of the most wonderful days of my life. It was an unforgettable demarcation point from which my whole life changed, almost as much as when I was born again. On that day I knew beyond any shadow of a doubt that I was no longer single but married.

This was far more than just a legal change in my status—my heart was changed on my wedding day. I already loved my wife to be, but from that day it was more than love—we were united as one. Our marriage has suffered many pressures but never once has it entered my mind that dissolving the marriage was an option. As a pilot I was often alone in foreign cities with an abundance of temptations, but by grace I never fell to them. I would like to say that I was kept by my commitment, but it took more than that. It was love for my wife and family more than commitment.

Commitment is important, but love is more powerful. Our gospel is tragically flawed if it does not accurately present the cross. Our discipleship is tragically flawed if we do not lead believers past the cross to a personal, intimate, love affair with Jesus. Commitment may only go as far as our will power, but a man or woman in love will never quit. Commitment and will power are virtues, just as self-control is listed as a fruit of the Spirit, but love is the greatest power because **"God is love" (I John 4:8).**

In Hebrews 6:1&2 we are exhorted: **"Therefore, leaving the elementary teaching about the Christ, *let us press on to maturity*, not laying again a foundation of repentance from dead works and of faith toward God, of instruction about washings, and laying on of**

hands, and the resurrection of the dead, and eternal judgment." First we must note here that this exhortation does not exhort us to leave the teachings about Christ, but rather the *elementary* teachings about Him.

We do not press on to maturity by leaving the teachings of Christ, but by taking hold of the advanced revelations of Him. Jesus is the Beginning and the End. He is everything. All things were made through Him, for Him, and all things will be summed up in Him. There is a point after the foundation has been properly laid, that we must go on to construct the rest of the building. However, that does not mean that we no longer have the foundation, but once it is laid we always have it with us.

Obviously, everything in our Christian life is built upon repentance and faith toward God. We will never receive anything from Him as a result of our own merit or maturity, but because of His blood. Once these truths have been properly secured in our foundation, we may go on to greater revelations of Christ, but everything else will be founded upon these truths and must be fastened to them if the building is to stand.

Marriage is a covenant so grand that it is deserving of the pomp and ceremony that we devote to it with our weddings. It is true that the wedding is not the marriage, but a ritual by which we commit ourselves to marriage, and such rituals are important. They help to impress upon us the seriousness of the covenant we are making. Our covenant is not the marriage, but it is the foundation upon which the marriage is built, and one that is designed to promote the love that will constitute a strong marriage.

Baptism is our spiritual wedding to the Lord. It is a grand and powerful act. It is one that He decreed and it cannot be improved upon to accomplish its purpose. Yet, the modern altar call, that is not even biblical, has supplanted baptism as the ceremony of commitment. This could well be one of the primary reasons why "decisions" for the Lord often remain shallow.

In the New Testament, when someone made the commitment to follow Jesus they were immediately baptized. If water was not close an immediate search was made for it so that the new convert could be immersed. Baptism is not our spiritual life, it is not our communion, it is a ritual. However, keeping the sanctity of this God ordained ritual can have a lot to do with the quality of the conversion—which is our commitment to no longer live for ourselves, but for Jesus, married to Him.

An important part of repairing the spiritual nets so that they can hold the catch includes restoring baptism to its rightful place. Will it be inconvenient to always immediately baptize those who give their lives to Jesus? Yes. But our addiction to convenience has been a primary factor causing us to compromise both the gospel and our own spiritual lives. Somewhere this addiction must be cast off, so why not at the beginning? If we are going to compel converts to submit to Jesus as Lord, how are we justified in so easily abandoning his directives?

Tending His Sheep

The biblical term for conversion is to be "born again." There are probably few creatures in this world more helpless than a newborn human being. A mother's care for her newborn is almost a continuous endeavor. The same is true of a newborn Christian. Few will survive if they are just fed once or twice a week.

When there is true revival all the saints want to do is meet together, because there is nothing in this world more exciting than a move of God. This is also the Holy Spirit's way of ensuring the care of the new believers who come to Jesus during times of revival. However, what about those who come when there is no revival? Overall, many more people come to the Lord between the waves of revival than during the revivals themselves, which are usually very short-lived. There are also probably far more converts who slip through the nets when there is no revival going on than when there is.

I have been credited (and accused) of being one who has had a lot to do with awakening the church to the impending harvest. This was a burden that was given to me and I am very thankful for the seemingly world-wide awakening to these great times that are upon us. The subject of revival is one of my greatest loves. However, one of my greatest concerns has also been much of the church's overemphasis on revival. Some have become like the cripple sitting by the pool waiting for someone to stir the waters, while the Son of God Himself, is standing right next to them. Regardless of how clearly we are able to perceive impending events, we will not be ready for them if we fail to see what the Lord wants to do with us TODAY.

The fields are already white for harvest. Many are already reaping. There are genuine revivals igniting in many countries now. Before the end these waves will sweep over every place, but if they are not yet in our city or locality, let us use the time wisely, drawing closer to the Lord, and equipping the saints for the work of the ministry for which they will all be called. One way that we can do this is to treat each new believer with whose care we are entrusted as if he were a hundred. If we are faithful with the few the Lord will then give us the hundreds. Presently the Holy Spirit is searching the earth for such faithful shepherds. The authority given to the faithful will be increased.

Almost every new believer will require day and night fellowship and teaching for a period of time. If you are a pastor, and reading this causes a dread to come over you because you cannot possibly comprehend this massive endeavor, that is a sure indication that you have not properly equipped the saints who you have been given to equip. Jesus said, **"my yoke is easy, and my burden is light…" (Matthew 11:30)**, because He has given every one of us many others to help us carry this responsibility. A primary reason for excessive burdens in ministry is our own failure to share the burdens with those He has given us for that purpose.

Tending the Lord's sheep does not just mean keeping them all in a big sheep pen and throwing them some food a couple of times a week—it means turning the sheep into shepherds! Won't this threaten your job? Of course. But you will never get a true promotion in the Spirit until you have worked your way out of your present position. You are not a true pastor unless your ministry is producing other pastors. You are not a true teacher unless you are producing other teachers. Those who are not reproducing their own ministry in others are "seedless fruit."

The Three Levels Of Ministry

The Lord provided ministry on basically three levels: He had food for the multitudes, then the twelve, then the three. During the first part of His ministry He devoted most of His attention to the multitudes. However, as soon as He had identified those who would be the leaders of His church, He began to give most of His attention to them. A truly balanced ministry will always gravitate toward this same pattern—giving more attention to developing those who can take their place than to the multitudes.

Amazingly, as soon as just one of His disciples received the revelation of who Jesus was, the Lord gave the keys to the kingdom to that disciple and started making plans to leave them! This shocked Peter to the point that He rebuked the Lord, who rebuked him back for not setting his mind of God's interests, but man's. When the Lord went to the cross and began His departure from this realm, His disciples looked anything but ready to assume leadership of the church—they had deserted Him! However, the Lord never took the keys of the kingdom back from Peter, or His commissions from the others. He fully trusted the Holy Spirit to make these men into what they should be, and to build a church against which the gates of hell could not prevail.

Jesus was unquestionably the greatest Leader of all time. If He could trust His eternal work to a church that was in such a condition, how much more should we be able to trust those we are leading with responsibility, also? Those who are too afraid of potential mistakes to properly delegate authority may be able to get a lot done by themselves, but they are failures as spiritual leaders.

Seminaries Of The Future

The only seminary that the apostles knew was "on the job training." The only seminary that their disciples knew was "on the job training." Some seminaries and Bible schools have added a great deal of depth and richness to the church. However, they have also weakened the church to the degree that they have eclipsed the Lord's own ordained method for preparing ministries—personal discipleship. This must be recovered in the days to come or the church will be tragically unprepared for what is coming.

Education is fundamental to Christianity. Education is illumination, or light, and we are called to be the light of the world. The kind of education that is provided in seminaries can help greatly to prepare one for ministry, if it is true to the Scriptures. Seminaries do allow for some students to be discipled to a degree by some of the finest teachers. However, if we really want to be a biblical people we must again view the local church as the ultimate seminary. This will become a major move of the Holy Spirit, and will accelerate as we progress toward the end of this age.

Indeed, the Lord physically left the church in what appeared to be a disastrous condition. He did this because He trusted the Holy Spirit. One of the primary reasons why the church today is so weak and unprepared for the times is not under-preparation, but *over-preparation*. We are requiring our future leaders to be much more than what God requires, because we do not trust the Holy Spirit enough. As the time gets shorter, we will have less and less time to equip future leaders. We will have to give them greater and greater responsibilities with increasingly less training. However, the Holy Spirit will make up the difference, and that will make these leaders some of the greatest the world has ever known. His grace is sufficient. His strength is still made perfect in weakness.

Reaching The World From Home

The Scriptures give the most effective strategy for evangelizing the world *while staying right at home*, yet this strategy has been almost completely neglected by the church. God's plan for evangelizing the world was the simplicity of showing hospitality to foreigners, to love them and then teach them the ways of God. The Lord first gave this strategy to the children of Israel while they were in the wilderness:

> **For the Lord your God is the God of gods and the Lord of lords, the great, the mighty and the awesome God, who does not show partiality nor take a bribe.**
>
> **He executes justice for the orphan and the widow,** *and shows His love for the alien*, **by giving him food and clothing.**
>
> *So show your love for the alien*, **for you were aliens in the land of Egypt (Deuteronomy 10:17-19).**

Here we see that God loves the foreigners and wants to give them provisions. The Lord uses His people as extensions of His grace. He therefore commands His people to love foreigners.

America is a nation built on the immigration of foreigners. Some came to America because they were persecuted. Others came just seeking a better life. America's openness and hospitality to foreigners is one of the primary reasons for our many blessings. A nation's health is dependent upon one thing—pleasing God—and He will provide for those who love and serve those whom He loves and wants to serve.

The Lord has a special place in His heart for the poor, widows and orphans, and for foreigner, basically because they are all in need and are lonely. Loneliness was the very first thing that God said was not good (see Genesis 2:18). If we love and care for those that the Lord wants to care for we become the channels for His provision and blessing. Foreigners in our midst give us a unique opportunity to serve the Lord, but He wants us to give them more than just food and clothes, as stated in Deuteronomy 31:12:

> **Gather the people together, men and women and little ones,** *and the stranger who is within your gates,* **that they may hear and that they may learn to fear the Lord your God and carefully observe all the words of this law (NKJV).**

He wants us to love the foreigner so that we can teach them His ways. Just as He told Israel in Deuteronomy chapter 10 to love the foreigner, and then in chapter 31 to teach them His ways, we must love someone before we can teach them. We cannot do His work until we have His love. When we have His love we will be given all that we need to do His work. As these two scriptures indicate, His work will involve providing for their needs, and teaching them His ways.

Many foreigners still come to our land each year, often destitute and lonely. Many of them have been driven from their homes and families. The Lord has a special sympathy for such and He will bless those who minister to them. The Lord said that, when He returns He will divide between the sheep and the goats, taking the sheep with Him to eternal life and sending the goats to eternal judgment. The only difference distinguishing the sheep and goats was that the sheep visited Him while He was in prison, gave Him food to eat and water to drink, and clothes for covering and they *took Him in when He was a foreigner* (see Matthew 25:31-46). When they asked Him when they did these things He replied that it was when they did it to His brothers.

The goats were those who did not visit Him in prison, did not give Him food, water, clothes or take Him in when He was a foreigner, because they did not do this for His brothers. Are we likewise missing Him by neglecting those He sends to us? This is a most serious issue because we will be judged as sheep or goats according to how we receive those He *sends to us*.

Continuing The Blessing

Lets look at another significant, but often overlooked, exhortation that the Lord gave to Israel:

> **At the end of every third year you shall bring out all the tithe of your produce in that year, and shall deposit it in your town.**
>
> **And the Levite, because he has no portion nor inheritance among you, *and the alien, the orphan and the widow* who are in your town, shall come and eat and be satisfied, in order that the Lord your God may bless you in all the work of your hand which you do (Deuteronomy 14:28-29).**

Here we see that every third year the tithe was to be shared with the foreigner, the fatherless and the widow. This was to provide for their needs *so that the Lord would continue to bless the work of the land*. After Israel had been faithful to set aside the tithe and give it to the Levite, the foreigner, the fatherless and the widow, they were then told to call upon God to look down upon them and their faithfulness in this in order to bless their land and make it flow with milk and honey (see Deuteronomy 26:12-15). Many have been faithful to preach the tithe, but are they using the tithe properly? Could this be why many who give and receive tithes are still not blessed?

To take the tithe every third year and give it to the Levites in the towns (full time ministries), foreigners, widows and orphans means that most congregations would only be able to live on two thirds of their tithe income for their expenses. That would mean that many church buildings would probably have to be a third smaller. Would this be a great tragedy? I have been in many local churches and rarely have I ever seen one more than two thirds full. However, this would probably not be a factor. The congregations that were using the tithes properly would probably be receiving so much grace and anointing that they would be many times larger than we are now. The Lord will bless those who are caring for the ones He wants to care for. To provide that care we don't need buildings nearly as much as we need the anointing.

This issue was not just for those under the Old Covenant. When Paul outlined the qualifications for leadership in the church one such requirement was that an elder be one who showed hospitality to foreigners (In Titus 1:8 this is sometimes translated simply one who shows hospitality but the literal translation is "a friend to aliens"). How many churches today consider this a main characteristic of those appointed to leadership positions? It is obviously important to the Lord, and will help determine the amount of blessing and anointing that will flow through that ministry.

Hospitality And Authority

True hospitality is one of the most basic demonstrations of genuine love, which is the foundation of all true ministry and spiritual authority. Our homes and families are usually our most prized possessions; to share them is to truly give of ourselves. That is why showing hospitality to foreigners is required of a man in a leadership in the church, which is called to be **"a house of prayer for all the nations"** (Mark 11:17).

The Lord ordained that His people would be a generous and hospitable people because He, Himself, is generous and hospitable. His people are to reflect His nature and hospitality is a reflection of the Lord's generosity. Hospitality is a means of teaching the world about Him. As well as a representation of the Lord's nature, hospitality is a key element of His strategy for the coming harvest.

The Strategy

The Lord is now preparing hundreds of thousands of families to open their homes to Him by opening them to His people. This grace of hospitality will open many to the gospel and teachings of the Lord. Great evangelistic and teaching ministries will be born from couples who begin to open their homes in this way.

These should begin to prepare spiritually for the harvest like some might prepare in the natural for an impending war. Instead of setting aside food, clothing and other provisions, these should begin setting aside spiritual food, clothing and provisions. Now is the time to begin stockpiling Bibles, Bible Studies, books and basic teaching tapes. Now is the time to learn how to heal the sick, cast out demons, and help lay a solid spiritual foundation in a new believer's life.

As stated, in previous revivals a high percentage of new believers were quickly lost again to the world. Many of these would have a genuine conversion but, like newborn infants who are completely dependent on the care of their parents, new believers are dependent on the church to provide for them spiritually until they are mature enough to take care of themselves. When revival has come in the past the church has seldom been prepared for it. This time can be different. The Lord is right now moving on mature, stable men and women of God to prepare to raise these new spiritual infants so they will not be lost again to the world.

Now is the time for us to all prepare by sinking our own roots deeper into the word of God and by developing our personal relationships with Him. We must know what we believe in and know how to teach it. In areas to which you feel called, but in which you feel inadequate to now serve, go to your pastors and teachers and ask them for training. What they begin to do for you they will probably also do for others. If you cannot find help in your local congregation, there are now conferences and seminars being offered throughout the body of Christ that address almost every area of ministry. There are also many quality home study courses. If you care enough to invest in the purposes of the Lord, He will invest more in you. We are promised that if we seek, we will find.

Some are called to teach groups of new believers once a week; some will be devoting every night to this work. It will be a mammoth task but it is the Lord's work; He will give us the grace and strength to accomplish it. When we take His yoke upon us we actually find rest and refreshment instead of the exhaustion we might expect. There are few efforts that so quicken and awaken the church as the ingathering of new believers.

Let us prepare now, before the flood comes. First we must get our own lives in order. We must get rid of the excess baggage in our lives. We must eliminate the compromise and the sin which may have crept in. The Lord said that after one has been taught he "becomes like his teacher." These are the King's own children whom He is entrusting us to teach. Let us not only be careful how we teach them, but how we ourselves live; our lives will be teaching them just as much as the knowledge we impart.

If we are absorbing two hours of television and ten minutes of the word each day, the quality of our ministry will reflect it. It is a truth that "you are what you eat;" we do reap what we sow. If we sow that which is true life into our hearts, that is the fruit that we will bear. We certainly would not give a king's children spoiled or poison food; how much more careful should we be with the Lord's own children. We must give them the best, because as we are doing unto them, we are doing unto Him.

The Holy Spirit Challenge

The Holy Spirit is about to challenge all mature believers with the same challenge that He gave to Peter before His ascension. He will be asking us repeatedly if we love Him. If we say "yes," we must be ready to feed and tend His sheep. I appreciate my wife's affection for me, but it would not mean much if she let my children go hungry, or did not take care of their other needs. We can attend every meeting and sing every song with passion, but we will still be a goat if we do not give Him water when He is thirsty, and food when He is hungry; and if when He comes to us as a foreigner, we do not take Him in.

Chapter Eleven

Notable Spiritual Trends

When the Lord spoke to the seven churches in Revelation He had a different message for each one. These were all churches that existed during the same period of time and in the same geographic region, yet they all needed a different word. We must understand that the Lord is doing many different things in His church at the same time. Therefore it is wrong for us to impose on everyone else what the Lord may be doing in us. The following trends currently exist, or will be forthcoming in the church. I am sharing them for the purpose of perspective only, and do not want to imply that He is doing all of these things with everyone.

Leadership Training

We may not consider leadership training as a movement, but it will become one the most popular new trends in the church. Like many other trends, some will think that this is the answer to all of the church's problems, while others will view it as a great threat. It will have the answers to some problems, but it will also create some others.

There are principles of leadership that can be related to everyone in authority, both spiritual or secular. Studying these can enhance our effectiveness as leaders. However, there are many leadership principles that relate to secular authority which have no place in spiritual authority. This is where the problems will arise. Much can be accomplished in terms of expansion and organization using these secular principles. Although having the appearance of success and advancement, these principles accomplish little spiritually.

We are not leaders unless we are going somewhere, and someone is willing to follow us. Everyone wants to be identified with success, and many people will follow anyone who seems to be going somewhere. A major problem with indiscriminate leadership training is that the principles can be used to lead people just about anywhere. Hitler, Stalin and Mao were all effective leaders who understood and used "good" leadership principles.

Spiritual leadership, founded upon true spiritual authority, is very different from the world's form of leadership. Confusing the two can cause great problems. Our goals must not be just success, but doing the Lord's will. We can preempt the problems caused by the misuse of leadership principles in the church by teaching solid foundational principles of spiritual authority and how it contrasts with secular authority.

One powerful idol in the church that must be cast down is the "growth god." The Lord does care about numbers, as He desires for all men to be saved and come to the knowledge of the truth. However, when growth becomes a goal for its own sake, we often depart from the path of obedience. Even the Lord's own followers sometimes departed from Him when He had to take difficult stands. Those who are walking in true spiritual authority will not be overly encouraged by growth, or overly discouraged when the pruning comes, and it always does.

This growth god has been the root cause of the destruction of many congregations, movements, and ministries. If we will focus on growing in faith, in the knowledge of the Son of God, in wisdom and anointing, then we will grow in the proper timing and way. Such growth has a solid foundation and does not have to be maintained by human strength, but will be sustained by the Holy Spirit. In such growth there is total rest for our souls, and the bearing of fruit that will remain.

The Great Repositioning

There are many anointed ministries that are bearing little fruit because they are not in the right place spiritually. Some are evangelists who are trying to be pastors. Others are pastors who are trying to be prophets, etc. The Lord is about to reposition those who have drifted from their true callings, and give them a clear revelation of the sphere of authority that has been appointed to them. Others are out of the geographical will of the Lord. These too will be helped as the Lord is about to open the doors for them to be properly positioned.

There are spiritual jurisdictions similar to jurisdictions in the realm of human government. Just as a policeman in Atlanta does not have authority to make arrests in Amsterdam, we only have authority within the spiritual and geographical realm of our commission. The apostle Paul confirmed this when he told the Corinthians: **"But we will not boast beyond our measure, but within the measure *of the sphere which God apportioned to us* as a measure, to reach even as far as you" (II Corinthians 10:13).**

When we venture beyond the realm of our authority we can work hard but little will be accomplished. This has been a major cause for the ineffectiveness of many leaders in the church. If the apostle Paul, whom every demon in hell respected, was careful to stay within his sphere, how much more must we? In this matter the Lord has given us much tolerance in the past, but the consequences of being out of His will may become increasingly grave in the times ahead.

One of the primary factors that has caused many Christians to depart from the spiritual or geographical will of the Lord is our tendency to be led by our own needs, or those of others. Jesus never responded to human needs—He only did what He saw the Father doing. He had compassion for the problems of others, and He could have solved all of them, but He was careful to only follow the Father's leading. We must do the same. This tendency to take the people's yokes instead of the Lord's has caused much failure and burnout in the ministry. The Lord's yoke is easy, but no human can carry the yokes of the people without suffering terrible consequences.

Others have departed from the will of God because they responded to positions or places that offered greater financial rewards, visibility or influence. Such motives are in conflict with the Spirit, and when we are led in this way we will almost always begin to divert from the will of God. There is no amount of money or fame that is worth sacrificing the peace that comes from knowing that we are in God's will.

If this section has touched your heart, and you believe that in some way you have drifted from the will of God in your life, grace is now being extended to you. The way that we get back on the right road is to go back to where we missed the turn. I do not mean by this that you must return to a previous position, or geographical location, but that you repent of that which caused you to make the wrong turn.

To repent is to not only feel sorry about our sin, but to change our way of thinking and acting. We can go back to where we made the wrong turn, but if we have not changed our way of thinking we will only make the same mistake again. We must take every thought captive and make them all obedient to Christ. We are no longer our own, we are His bondservants. Bondservants cannot just decide to do what they want to do; they belong to another. If we do not live our lives in fundamental obedience to the Lord, we will drift continually out of His will.

The Joy Of The Lord

There is a great move of the Holy Spirit that is now touching almost every corner of the earth. It is evidenced by spontaneous outbreaks of "holy laughter." Though some individuals and congregations have become known as vessels through whom this is being released, it is happening in many places that have not even heard of these ministries. It is a spontaneous move of the Holy Spirit. Many are now moving about, by the Holy Spirit, casting sparks that are resulting in the fires of restoration and renewal.

There are "signs and wonders," but this is one sign that has many people wondering. Like every new move of the Holy Spirit in the church, many will judge it as being nothing more than a fad. For others it encompasses everything that God is doing today. Both of these extreme positions are in jeopardy of missing what the Lord is trying to do through this move. This may not be the main thing that the Lord is doing in His church today, but it is something that He is doing, and He has a very good reason for it.

Just as road signs give us directions, the signs given by the Spirit are for the purpose of giving directions. I once heard a person who had just moved to Atlanta say, "I appreciate those giant signs that tell you which way to get to I-85, but I am just as thankful for those little signs that let you know that you are *still on* I-85!" Likewise, some spiritual signs are meant to point us to the right road;

others are meant to let us know that we are still on the right road.

In one sense this holy laughter is the "sign of Sarah." She laughed when she was told by the Lord that she would have a son. Therefore, when she did, she named him Isaac, which means "laughter." It is now time for the church to give birth to "Isaac," the child of promise that will be the last day ministry. The Lord blessed Ishmael (representing the work originating in the flesh) and made him a great nation. The Lord has blessed many things that the church has initiated wrongly, but He cannot inhabit them. He will not use these for the fulfillment of His promises. The last day ministry of the church must be born by the will of God, in His timing, and by His Spirit. This represents the "Isaac ministry," and it will soon be with us.

Another reason for this special anointing of joy is found in Deuteronomy 28:47-48: **"Because you did not serve the Lord your God with joy and a glad heart, for the abundance of all things, therefore you shall serve your enemies …"** The failure to maintain the joy of the Lord is one of the primary reasons why Christians go into bondage, falling to the yokes of either legalism or license. The Lord is pouring out a special anointing of joy to help deliver us from these yokes that we have come under so that we can move again in His perfect will.

Nehemiah, after rebuilding the walls of Jerusalem and calling for a celebration of the Feast of Tabernacles, declared **"Do not be grieved for the joy of the Lord is your strength" (Nehemiah 8:10).** The Feast of

Tabernacles was the last feast of the Jewish calendar year. It was also called The Feast of Ingathering, and was a prophetic type of the harvest that will mark the end of this age. We will need a special anointing of the joy of the Lord to fulfill our last day mandate as the church. The world is coming into its time of greatest darkness, while right in the midst of it the church will be celebrating a great feast, with great joy. This is the table that has been prepared for us in the very presence of our enemies.

Nehemiah also spoke this charge to maintain the joy of the Lord just prior to leading the people into a time of heart wrenching repentance. We, too, are about to enter a period of deep repentance. The Lord is laying a foundation of joy so that we can endure this great repentance and not fall into the bondage of legalism.

It is interesting that in this "revival of laughter" there seem to be just as many people weeping as there are laughing, in the same meetings. Some individuals go from a supernatural weeping to a supernatural laughter, or vice versa. This is not confusion; the Lord is obviously doing both Himself. The Holy Spirit is groaning and travailing, yet the Scriptures also say that the Lord "… **sits in the heavens and laughs**" **(Psalm 2:4).** How could one who views the whole world, with both the victories and joys of His children, and the terrible darkness and evil, help but do both? As He is sharing His emotions with us, the issue is, are we being touched by the heart of God, or are we just getting caught up in the emotions of those around us? The church is called to be "the pillar and support of the truth," and there can be no place for falsehood.

March For Jesus

The March for Jesus has done much to stimulate interchange between churches, and to help deliver congregations from the prison of their own buildings. However, it too is facing a crisis. If it does not shift gears and accelerate into a new level of vision and strategy, it will soon brake to a stop. The Lord is giving an invitation to go forward, mobilizing an army of intercessors and evangelists for cities.

Cell Groups

The Cell Group Movement was also initiated by the Holy Spirit and will continue as a major thrust in the church. This is a crucial strategy for preparing the church for the harvest. It will also help to restore the ministry of the church to its proper foundations—building people.

Some extremes in the movement will also begin to manifest that will have the potential to injure many churches. Such are the growing pains that are experienced by almost every important movement in the church. Some will be tempted to react to the whole movement and discard it because of these extremes. That will be as costly to them as the extremes are to those who embrace them. There are many facets to this strategy that have not yet been revealed. *The downfall of any movement begins when it stops moving, or closes itself to increased wisdom for the strategy it was given.* This usually happens when the "pride of Mary" is able to take root in the leaders. Mary thought that because she had given birth to Jesus she therefore had a right to control Him.

This is an important movement, but it is not something that He is doing with everyone. By no means should it ever become an issue that we allow to divide us from others in the body of Christ. Without grace, tolerance and patience, this movement will soon suffer a tragic derailment, which would be a serious blow to the preparation of the church for her last day ministry. With grace and wisdom, it will be one of the most effective strategies for accomplishing this preparation.

Children And Youth

The Lord views every child given to a family, or congregation, as a most valuable talent that He has entrusted to them. Many of these "talents" are being buried in programs that do nothing more than babysit them while the parents are spiritually fed. The congregations who wisely devote themselves to the spiritual growth and care of the children will be blessed and prospered with greater anointing and resources in all they are called to do. Those who do not will see even what they have, given to others.

Many of the most anointed of the last day ministries are now children. Many already have the authority and power to make a difference in the church. We must be open to let them take their proper places as members of the body. However, we must keep in mind that the Lord does not want us to make them like us; He wants to make us like them. They are the ones who know how to enter the kingdom.

Like Daniel's friends, Shadrach, Meshach and Abednego, there is a generation of young people who will not eat the food offered to the idols of their generation, nor bow down and worship them. They also will be confronted and tested by the conjurers, the sorcerers and wise men of this age, but will be found to have ten times more wisdom than all of them. The Lord Himself will walk with them in the midst of the fire and they will not be burned. They will stand as a witness and will turn many to the worship of the only God of heaven and earth, and will cause some of the world's most powerful leaders to worship Him. Like Daniel, every attack against them will only result in greater authority and higher esteem being given to them in the sight of all.

Prayer

Every ministry is an aspect and outreach of the Lord's own ministry. A teacher is one through whom Jesus the Teacher reaches to give His people knowledge and understanding. A pastor is one whom the Chief Shepherd uses to touch the needs of His people, etc. *The intercessor is one who has especially identified with the prayer ministry of Jesus* "Who ever lives to intercede."

Everyone is called to do the work of the evangelist, to share Christ with the lost, but that does not make everone an evangelist by commission. Every believer will at times share biblical insights, but that does not make everyone a teacher by commission, etc. Everyone is supposed to pray and intercede, but not all are called to the ministry of intercession. Those who are have a very high calling, but also a difficult one.

There is very little recognition or understanding of this ministry within the church, but it may also be one of the most important. The Lord said that His house would be "a house of prayer for all the peoples," yet presently this might be one of the most neglected ministries of all. If the Lord has determined that His house would be a house of prayer, then why do we not support intercessors like other staff members? If we gave prayer the importance that God obviously gave it, one must wonder how radically different the church might be.

Why is prayer so important to God? Doesn't He already know our needs before we ask Him? If He does then why does He want us to ask Him? Prayer is not for His sake but ours. Unfortunately, if we did not have to pray to receive from God it is likely that He would get very little attention from us at all.

Jesus prayed throughout His life, but He did not begin His ministry of intercession until after the cross. The power of true intercession is found in sacrifice, which is the most profound expression of love. Only those who love will lay down their lives. Intercession is a sacrifice that requires the laying down of our lives and interests to identify with the needs of others. Prayer and intercession were typified by incense in the temple rituals, and this incense was offered upon an *altar*. An altar had only one purpose—sacrifice. True intercession is a spiritual sacrifice, an expression of love which moves the heart of God.

There are many great prayer movements in the world today. Even so, this emphasis is about to dramatically increase throughout the church. It will be recognized that those who have authority with God are accomplishing much more than those who have authority with men. Intercession is about to become a holy obsession in the church. These great prayer movements will result in such extraordinary advances for the church, and deliverance for the world, that the world's great and mighty will come to the church for prayer. Even the public schools in the United States will beg for prayers to be made in their halls again. The whole world will know that "the God of the Christians" is the one Who answers prayer.

Spiritual Warfare

Spiritual warfare has been credited with igniting significant revivals. There have also been noteworthy results with some who have sought to change the spiritual climate over their cities, and even some nations. Likewise, as with every movement, there have also been noteworthy mistakes, abuses and foolishness related to spiritual warfare. There will be a time of increasing controversy and testing in order to mature this movement and prepare it for the mainstream of the church. It will be as it flows into the mainstream that it will become properly balanced, and will help release the full power and authority of the spiritual weapons given to the church.

The Charismatic Renewal

During one of the most difficult and confusing periods in our country's history, when the "counter-cultural" forces were being unleashed to challenge almost every foundation of society, the Charismatic Renewal arose with great power to give direction and vision to a generation. This movement rose up to meet a great onslaught of the enemy and won many great victories.

The Charismatic Renewal resulted in more salvations, more churches being renewed, more ministries and missionaries being released, than any other renewal, revival, or movement in history. This renewal also spawned devastating mistakes and failures, but it has nevertheless been one of the greatest blessings to ever come upon the church. Now the Lord is going to redeem many of the mistakes that were made, turning them into demonstrations of His power of redemption.

We must not confuse this redemption with the understanding that these were in fact mistakes. However, the Lord wants to teach us His way of handling mistakes. The Lord does rebuke and chastise without compromise, but He also does so in a way that results in restoration. In one of the most extraordinary examples of His heart for redemption, He even "gave Jezebel time to repent" (see Revelation 2:21). Even when Ahab, the husband of the Old Testament Jezebel and one of the most evil kings in Israel's history, humbled himself and repented, the Lord immediately embraced him, healed him, and restored him. Humility before God is one of the greatest powers on earth, because God gives His grace to the humble. However, it is also God's grace that brings the needed correction in our lives to keep us on course.

Even though the "glory days" of the Charismatic Renewal are now in the past, some of the great ministries from this movement will again take center stage for a time. They will use this platform to sum up the victories, the mistakes, and the vision of this movement as a powerful blessing of wisdom to the next spiritual generation. Some will even remain as "Joshuas and Calebs" to lead the next generation. Others will then pass with great honor, because the Lord wants to honor this movement.

The Third Wave

The Third Wave Movement has made significant contributions to the church's advancement over the last decade. It can be credited with helping whole new sections within the body of Christ to become open to the supernatural gifts of the Spirit and power ministry.Through it significant contributions have been made in the areas of worship, cell groups, spiritual warfare, helping to release many effective new leaders into the church. This movement brought a fresh emphasis upon integrity during a difficult time in church history.

However, one subtle mistake threatens to bring this movement to a premature end.

In an attempt to disassociate itself from the Pentecostal and Charismatic movements, which were in the midst of making serious mistakes, a subtle disdain for those groups took root. We must remember the blessing of the commandment to honor our fathers and mothers was given so that we can "remain long upon the earth." Because the Third Wave movement, as a whole, did not properly honor their spiritual parents among the Pentecostals and Charismatics, but often ridiculed them, their time as a movement may be short.

This destiny can be avoided with repentance for this spiritual pride, and by a sincere devotion to properly honor those who have gone before them to make their own way straight. If this is not done, the Third Wave movement will quickly begin to whither, eventually being reduced to a mere footnote in church history.

Prophetic Restoration

A new wave of ministries is about to be released with extraordinary prophetic gifts. Others with revelatory gifting who were sidetracked because of controversy, or other problems, are about to get back on the fast track. This movement will then capture the attention of the entire church, and even civil authorities. However, this will bring a time of much greater danger for those called to this ministry, than the onslaught of the accuser that has dogged this movement. The controversy has only helped to purify and mature those who are about to be mightily used by the Lord. The enemy will try to use this acclaim to seduce the gifted with the *spirit of Balaam*, who was compelled to use his gifts for special interests.

For those who are faithful and obedient to the Holy Spirit, there will be continual and substantial increases to the anointing and authority with which they are trusted. For those who have tolerated sin, rejection, rebellion or bitterness, these sins will have an increasing power to cause stumbling in their lives. Because this ministry has a special place in preparing the bride for the coming of the King, He is jealous for those who prepare His bride to be pure themselves. Those called to this ministry who walk uprightly will have a significant part in helping all of the other ministries in the body of Christ rise to the stature, authority, and power to that which they have been called.

Apostolic Restoration

The apostolic ministry that opened the church age will be raised up at the end to complete it. The Lord is restoring the apostolic authority to the church, and soon this will become a major emphasis. There will be almost a general openness to this as men of true apostolic authority, with a true apostolic lifestyle, take their place in leadership.

The Lord blessed the Church of Ephesus saying, **"... you put to the test those who call themselves apostles, and they are not, and you found them to be false..." (Revelation 2:2).** There are, and will continue to be, many who call themselves apostles who are not. Most of these are not evil men, and some may actually be doing apostolic work. Even so, they have presumed for themselves a level of authority that the Lord has not given to them. If the church allows these to be called apostles who are not, there will be a devaluation of our spiritual currency.

However, the biblical stature of this ministry is *less* than what many idealists will presume it to be. Even the greatest apostle is an earthen vessel. Even the apostle Paul, who represents the essence of this ministry to many, sometimes came **"in weakness, and fear, and in much trembling…" (I Corinthians 2:3).** He confessed to the Galatians that his flesh had been a trial to them (see Galatians 4:13-14). The real apostle Paul would probably disappoint most of us today, as even the Lord Jesus Himself did to most of those who were looking for the Messiah. To receive a ministry, we must know men after the Spirit, and not after the flesh.

There is a blessing, as well as a need, for testing and discovering those who call themselves apostles but are not. Even so, there is also a blessing for identifying and receiving those who really are apostles. One must receive a prophet "in the name of a prophet" to receive a prophet's reward. Likewise one must receive an apostle in the name of an apostle to receive an apostle's reward. If we receive an apostle as just a teacher, that is all that we will get—teaching. But if we receive an apostle as an apostle, we will get the full benefit of his ministry.

The idealistic have always missed what the Lord was doing in their generation. They rejected the prophets, the Lord Jesus, the apostles to the early church, and every move of God since. Even Andrew Murray, who prayed for years for the outpouring of the Holy Spirit, rejected it when it came because it was not in the form that he had expected. In receiving the new apostolic movement, and apostolic influence in the church, we must not be idealistic, but biblical. Those who are gullible, and those who are idealistic, will both miss this move of God. The gullible will accept the false; the idealistic will reject the true.

The Post Modern Missionary Movement

The modern missionary movement has spread the gospel to countless multitudes over the last few centuries. However, many of our missionary strategies are still left over from colonial times, when transportation to parts of the world could take months. Because modern transportation is now so efficient, the need for individuals and families to relocate for long periods of time will be replaced by powerful new "impact teams."

Because of the way missions was often used as an excuse for exerting imperialistic strategies, missionaries are still often viewed by "host" countries as a threat to their culture to be resisted. However, the new missionary movement will have more in common with stealth bombers than their historic counterparts. They will hit their targets so hard and so fast that it will be hard for hostile governments and powers to even recognize the source of the explosions of the gospel. Missions that were once projected to take years, or even decades, will be accomplished in days. Just as individual stealth fighters in the Persian Gulf War were credited with doing the damage of 3,000 World War II bombers because of their accuracy, speed, and invisibility, the same will be true of the new missionary teams.

Right To Life

The Right to Life movement has greatly helped the church to understand and begin to confront one of the most important issues of our times. It has awakened and challenged many believers to take uncompromising stands for their convictions. For this we owe it much. Now this movement has come to an obvious crisis in its own life, and it is destined to fracture and drift into extremes. However, God's Right to Life movement will not die, but will arise from another source, and the rightful one—a powerful new women's movement. There it will come forth with such grace and wisdom that even its enemies will bow in respect.

Without repentance, the remnants of the old Right to Life movement will go seriously awry. On its present course, this movement will result in increasingly bitter division in both the church and the country. It will spark increasing violence, which will result in growing repression and the loss of religious freedom. It will also doom other righteous causes and political candidates. Fear of religious zealotry will grip the country to such a degree that it will cause moderates and the undecided to swing to opposite extremes; they will even be willing to deny Christians their basic liberties.

By falling to the use of carnal weapons and strategies, this movement is now playing into the enemy's strategy against the unborn, the church, and basic moral values. This movement's present strategies will almost all ultimately produce the opposite results of those that were intended.

As the movement itself begins to fracture it will be with poison like radioactive contamination, driving people into shelters to escape it. This is also part of the enemy's strategy to drive the church into obscurity. Instead of uniting the church it will divide it. Instead of activating lukewarm believers, it will deactivate many who had great zeal for the Lord. Instead of saving lives, it will end up destroying many more by driving them from the gospel.

The Right to Life movement has captured some of the most courageous and zealous believers in the church. Many of these have the potential to become great leaders, and are desperately needed by the body of Christ. However, many who come out of this movement will need long periods of "decontamination" before they will be safe for church leadership again. Human zealotry is one of the most difficult strongholds to be delivered from, taking considerable time and patience, which are qualities obviously lacking in zealots.

In spite of all of the mistakes, the lessons learned from the Right to Life movement will prove valuable for the last day ministry of the church. The power of demonstration can accomplish a little, but demonstrations of power will accomplish much more. The Lord does care deeply for the unborn, and He does want to save them. He also wants to save their mothers and fathers. If we will give ourselves more to helping people to be reborn, many more of these babies will have a better chance to be born.

Men's Movements

The emerging men's movement in America has been a fresh stream of new life to flow through the church. It has already done much for the renewal of the church, and the strengthening of families against the devastating satanic assaults of the last few decades. This movement is anointed for continued growth, in numbers as well as power.

The enemy has also placed three major stumbling blocks before this movement. One satanic strategy is to sidetrack it, allowing "spiritual special interest groups" to divert its energy and influence for their own, more narrow, causes. Another strategy is to use commercial interests to gain influence in order to divert its momentum. The third, is from political interests trying to do the same.

This movement is far more than "God's answer to the feminist movement." Even so, it will greatly overshadow the feminist movement as a spiritual force. With sensitivity to the strategy of the Lord, it will impact areas of society that other spiritual movements have been unable to penetrate, giving birth to some of the most effective strategies for the inner-city and racial problems of America, and then the world.

Women's Movements

After some years of pruning, many Christian women's groups are about to grow dramatically, in numbers as well as anointing. Much of this numerical growth will come through evangelism as the Lord turns thousands of small women's fellowships into powerful evangelistic teams. Others will become mighty in intercession and spiritual warfare, and will help spark great revivals and spiritual advances.

It will also be Christian women who will be the light that does much to open Islam to the gospel. Both Moslem men and women will be moved by the power and grace of these women. This power will be found in the dignity and beauty found in true, godly submission, which is fueled by love, not fear. Everything that churches invest in these fellowships will produce great dividends, as women's ministries in the church will become one of her richest resources.

It will be the women's movements in the church through which God's most effective strategy against abortion will arise. That these will be led by women will in itself give them much more credibility than previous pro-life movements. Because they will be led by women of such dignity and grace, it will cause even their most vehement enemies to show them deference, and will win many converts from other feminist movements. Through these movements both womanhood and motherhood will be raised to the level of honor and respect that they deserve. This will greatly impact the church's fruitfulness in both bringing forth spiritual births, and raising her spiritual children properly.

Ultimately these new Christian women's movements will diffuse the political clout of The National Organization for Women and other feminist organizations. However, it is a snare of the enemy for these to be diverted and used for political power themselves. Those who gravitate toward political power will lose their spiritual power proportionately.

When both men and women take their rightful place in the church, the church will take its rightful place in the world. These movements will do much to raise the church to her ultimate stature and beauty, which our glorious Savior deserves from His bride.

Summary

All of these movements are meant to contribute to the River of Life, but they themselves are not that river. It is imperative that we stay in the river and not be tempted to turn and follow a tributary. Even though the Holy Spirit is compared to the wind (see John 3), we are not supposed to be blown about by every new wind of doctrine. We must learn to let the winds blow, not resisting the Holy Spirit, but allowing them to refresh us and help us while we stay on the course where we have been called to walk.

After the church has been blown back and forth by many winds of doctrine over the last few decades, there is now a maturity and stability that will help us to properly relate to the new and powerful movements that are coming to help us. We must always keep our attention upon the Lord to follow Him and not movements. We are called to grow up "into the Head," not into a new teaching or trend. All of these movements and teachings can help us do this if we keep them in proper perspective.

Chapter Twelve

War And Glory

In August of 1993, I had a vision of the church. It was represented as an island in the middle of a sea. There were many different types of buildings all over this island, each of which I understood to represent a different denomination or movement. These buildings seemed to clash with each other architecturally as there were very old ones next to very modern ones. There was a war going on between many of the buildings, and most of them looked like bombed out shells. People were still living in the buildings, but most were starving and wounded.

The Controlling Spirits

There were two dark spirits over the island directing this war. One was named Jealousy and the other one, Fear. They congratulated each other every time one of the buildings suffered damage, or people were wounded.

I then saw two powerful and frightening spirits rising over the sea. These became storms. One was named Rage and the other, Lawlessness. They were stirring up the sea and causing great waves to crash onto the island. Soon these storms became so large that they seemed even more threatening to the island than the war.

I felt that the people in the city had to be warned about these storms, and several apparent watchmen were trying to do this, but no one would listen to them. The people only debated and argued about whether the watchmen should be trusted. This was remarkable because anyone who just looked up could see the storms for themselves.

These wars had left so many people wounded that the hospitals were fast becoming the largest buildings on the island. The hospitals were movements or denominations that had given themselves to healing the wounded. As these grew the other warring factions had no respect for them as being a place where even their own wounded were being cared for. Soon they became more resolved to destroy these hospitals as well as the other buildings.

As the war continued, even those who were not badly wounded had the appearance of phantoms, or became grotesquely deformed from the starvation and disease. Anytime a building received a supply of food, which would attract people, it would become a target. I could not comprehend how even a war could be so cruel—*and this was the church!*

In the midst of the battle men were still trying to add to their buildings, or to start new ones, but it was futile. Anytime one building would start to rise a little higher than the others, or anytime a new building was started, it would become the main target of all of the other buildings, and it would quickly be reduced to rubble.

I was then shown many powerful leaders who were conducting this war. All of them had the same word on their forehead: "Treachery." I was surprised that anyone would follow someone with that written on them, but they did. I was reminded of II Corinthians 11:20, **"For you bear with anyone if he enslaves you, if he devours you, if he takes advantage of you, if he exalts himself, if he hits you in the face."**

A Remnant

However, there were people who appeared as lights in almost every building. These lights refused to take part in the fighting, but spent their time trying to repair the buildings, or nurse the wounded. Even though it was impossible to keep up with the damage or the wounded, they did not stop trying.

It was also apparent that each of these lights had the power to heal wounds, and that power was increasing as they worked. Those who were healed became lights just as they were. It was obvious that these individuals who were committed to healing the wounded were now able to do more than the hospitals because of the ruthlessness of the attacks on the hospitals. Understanding this, the hospitals dispersed their people as "healing teams" which spread out across the island and moved into many of the other buildings.

There were also many small camps around the perimeter of the island. Some of these were involved in the war between the buildings. They wanted to destroy all of the buildings so that they could bring the people to their camps. The leaders of these camps had the same word "Treachery" written on their foreheads.

There were also few of these camps around the perimeter which were not involved in the war, and they too appeared as lights. These were also growing in authority, but it was a different authority than that of those with the healing powers. These had authority over events. They were praying to stop small battles, and to keep small storms away. Their prayers were becoming increasingly effective.

The two spirits over the city and the two storms became very intimidated by these small camps that were praying. It was obvious that these intercessory groups would soon have the authority to stop the big battles and big storms, which was obviously the source of agitation of these large spirits.

The Tragedy

There were multitudes of boats and ships all around the island that were waiting to enter the city as soon as the fighting stopped. Many of these boats were full of refugees from other wars, and many were wounded. There were also ships bearing kings, presidents and those who appeared wealthy and prosperous. These were all afraid of the storms, but they could not enter the city because of the fighting. Their groans and screams were so loud that I was surprised no one in the city could hear them. No one even seemed aware that the boats were out there.

In His Wisdom

Then I saw the Lord standing and watching. He was so glorious that I wondered why I had not seen Him before, or why everyone in the city did not stop to worship Him. To my amazement, no one was able to see Him. I then looked into the eyes of some of the people, and they were all so "bloodshot," from the dust of the city, that I was surprised that they could see anything at all. Their pupils were so small that I knew that they could only let in the smallest amount of light; and soon these people would be completely blind.

I then wondered why the Lord did not stop the fighting, but He seemed content to just watch. As if He had understood my thoughts, He turned and said to me, *"This is My church. These were the houses men tried to build for Me. I knocked on the door of each one, but they would not open to Me. I would have brought peace because I will only dwell in the city of peace."*

Then He turned and, indicating the people in the ships, He said: *"If I allowed all of these people to come to the city now they would just be used in the war. When their cries become louder than the war, I will build a place for them."*

Then He looked at me with great earnestness and said, *"I allowed this to happen so that it would never happen again!"* It is hard to convey the power of this statement, but it imparted to me a deep understanding that He allowed this conflict to continue out of profound wisdom. He then said, *"Until you understand this you cannot understand what I am about to do."*

When the cries of those in the boats became louder than the conflict in the city, the Lord gave a command and the sea was released. Great tidal waves arose and began to sweep across the island until they covered the buildings. The spirits that were storms joined the spirits over the island, and they all grew to almost double their previous size. Then the island completely disappeared under the darkness of the spirits and the raging sea.

The Lord did not move as this was happening. I knew that my only protection was to stand as close to Him as possible. I could not see anything but Him during this great storm. As I looked at His face I could see both hurt and resolve.

The House Of The Lord Is Built

Slowly, the storms died down and the tides receded. The individuals who were the lights in the buildings emerged and remained standing where the buildings had once been. Then the Lord, who had been on the edge of the island, moved to the center and said, *"Now I will build My house."*

All of those who were lights started turning toward the Lord. As they turned they became even brighter, and each group was changed into a living pillar right where they stood. Soon it became obvious that these pillars were the framework of a building which would cover almost the entire island

The pillars were different colors, shapes, and sizes. It was hard to understand how all of these, being so different, could work together as a single framework. However, the Lord seemed very pleased with each one. As the building took shape, the different pieces did eventually all fit together into a structure so harmonious that I could not imagine how even a single piece could have been left out.

My mind drifted to the incredible balance of the forces in the universe that were required to sustain our life on earth. If the earth's orbit around the sun drifted just the equivalent of 1/8th of an inch over a 32 mile distance we would either fry or freeze, yet this perfect balance was sustained by the gravitational forces from the planets and other heavenly bodies, as well as the sun. I thought of how the perfect balance of the gasses in our atmosphere, and the elements of the soil were all required to be in perfect harmony to support our life on earth. I remembered what I had read about the odds of just the gases in our atmosphere having come together as they did by chance, compared to the rarity with which these gases are found in the universe; this would defy computation by our greatest computers.

I then started to feel insecure as I realized how delicate all of these balances were in the natural. Knowing my thoughts, the Lord said, *"All of these balances are upheld by the word of My power. The balances are delicate, and the forces against them are now great, but my word is greater."*

Then I looked back at this glorious building that was the church. I knew that the harmony and balance wrought from the diversity in this building had reached a new level in the creation. I knew that even the angels were marveling at this great work. I understood that for this miracle to have arisen from the terrible darkness (and war was even greater than what had been brought forth when the Spirit had moved upon the formless void at the beginning), this church, this new creation, would be the crown upon all of the creations of God. This was the city for which Abraham had been searching, and all of those with true vision since.

Then again I began to feel insecure about how this incredible balance between so many of diverse nature could be sustained. Surely, some would start to go their own way and bring the whole building crashing down. This insecurity caused a great striving to rise up in my soul, and a gripping compulsion to do something, though I did not know what. Then the Lord arrested my heart by firmly grabbing both shoulders, saying, *"Remember the word of My power. It is I who have built this house and I will keep it. The striving that you feel is what brings the disharmony, and the divisions, and the collapse of those who do not abide in the power of My word."*

His words caused a great peace and strength to flood my soul. I knew that His word was much greater than I had ever perceived. He continued, *"You will never have peace if you look to the creation, even to the new creation that is My house. Look to Me. Look to My word. When you walk in My word you can walk anywhere and be at peace. When you walk in My word you can even walk on a stormy sea, because My word is greater than any storm."*

The People Come

Then the ships and boats all started landing on the island. There were multitudes of people. Each ship was from a different country or race of people. Soon I began to think that, even as large as it was, there were too many people for the building. Then the Lord looked at me and said very sternly, *"We will build as many rooms as we need—no one will be turned away."*

This was said so sternly that I resolved to never again consider turning people away as an option. I also pondered how the biggest problem before was how to get people to come to the buildings. Now the big problem was what to do with all of the people.

The Cemetery

When each ship arrived, the people on it were led straight to the Lord. He looked into the eyes of each one and said, *"If you trust Me you will die for Me."* When each said, "I will die for You," He immediately thrust His sword right through their heart. This caused very real pain in each one. To those who tried to avoid the sword it was obviously even more painful. To those who relaxed it did not seem to hurt as much.

These were then taken to a cemetery with the words "Obscurity" over the gate. I felt compelled to follow them. Those who had been stabbed were checked to see that they were really dead before they were buried. Some clung to life for a long time, and were laid off to one side. Quickly, those who were buried began to arise as lights just like those who had survived the storm. I noticed that they were not staying in their tombs the same length of time. Some of these had arisen before those who were clinging to life were even buried.

When I first looked at this cemetery it looked like a dreadful place and I did not think that it belonged at all on this now glorious island. As I left the cemetery I turned to look back at it, and it looked beautiful. I could not understand what was different. Then one of the workers said to me knowingly, "The cemetery has not changed—you have."

I again looked at the building and it was even more glorious than I had remembered. I then looked at the island and felt the same thing—it had become much more beautiful. I remembered the Scripture, **"Precious in the sight of the Lord is the death of His godly ones" (Psalm 116:15).** The worker, who was still looking at me, then said, "You have not died yet, but were changed just by being close to those who have. When you die you will see even more glory."

Those who were emerging as lights from the cemetery were each being led to their own place in the building, which would have their names on it. Some joined the walls, others joined the pillars, some became windows or doors. They remained people even after they became a part of the building. These really were "living stones."

I knew also that when they took their place "living" reached a higher level. Each life was magnified by the lives of all the others.

The Test

I returned to the Lord's side. Standing in His presence was so wonderful I could not imagine why anyone would not be willing to die for Him. Even so, many of the people coming from the ships did refuse. These would all back away from Him at the request. Many of these went back to the ships, some of which left and some of which remained in the harbor.

A few of the people who refused to die stayed on the island and were allowed to walk about freely, they were even allowed to enter the House of the Lord. They seemed to love and bask in the glory of it all. Many of these began to shine with a glory too, but they never had the glory within themselves—they only reflected what was coming from others.

As I was thinking that it was not right for these to be allowed to stay, the Lord said to me, *"My patience will win many of these, but even those that never give me their lives, I love and am pleased to let them enjoy My glory. Never turn away those who love My glory."* These really did enjoy the house, and enjoyed the presence of the Lord that radiated from the house, but they seemed timid, and retreated when the Lord Himself came close to them. Even so, the Lord loved them and rejoiced in their joy. I thought of Matthew 5:44-45:

> **"But I say to you, love your enemies, and pray
> for those who persecute you in order than you
> may be sons of your Father who is in heaven;
> for He causes His sun to rise on the evil and the
> good, and sends rain on the righteous and
> unrighteous."**

I then watched as those who had refused to die for the Lord begin to act as if His house were their own, and had been built for them. I wanted to be angry at their great presumption, but I could not feel anger even though I wanted to. I then understood that it was because I was standing so close to the Lord that I could not be mad. This forced me to make the decision to stay close to Him or move away so that I could be angry.

I was surprised that this was a difficult decision, that I would even consider wanting to move away from the Lord, but it honestly was. Out of fear at what was arising within me, I stepped closer to the Lord. He immediately reached out and grabbed me as though I were about to fall off of a cliff. As I looked behind me I was astonished to find that I had been on the very edge of a precipice, and had I taken that step away from the Lord to feel the anger, I would have stepped off of it.

He then said to me, *"In this house I can tolerate presumption more than that anger. That anger would start the war again."* I was then overwhelmed with the knowledge that I had not yet made the decision to die for Him either, and that I too had been presumptuously feeling possessive of both the house *and* the Lord. When I saw this great evil in my own heart I was appalled and immediately begged the Lord to destroy my evil heart with His sword.

Resurrection Life

When the Lord pierced My heart I was surprised to feel so little pain when it seemed to have been so hard on others. He then said, *"Those who request death die easier."* As I was fading from consciousness I remembered His statement in Matthew 21:44: **"And he who falls on this stone will be broken to pieces; but on whomever it falls, it will scatter him like dust."**

I did not remember being carried to the cemetery, but just as if no time at all had passed, I was emerging from it again. Now the glory of everything I saw was unspeakable. I looked at a rock and loved it. I looked at trees, the sky and clouds, and could not believe how wonderful they were. A sparrow seemed more glorious than any bird I had ever seen, and I marvelled at the great treasure that this little bird was. I wondered greatly at why I had not appreciated them like this before.

I then looked at the presumptuous people. Not only did I feel no temptation to be angry, I loved them so much I would have let each one pierce my heart again if it would have helped them. I then began to think of how blessed I was to be able to meet them and be with them. Now I actually wanted them to stay and could not even comprehend how I was ever tempted to be angry at them—they were much greater treasures than the sparrow!

The Betrayer

I then saw one who I knew to be a Judas, a betrayer. I did not fear him but I knew he had power to damage the building. I knew that he wanted so badly to be a part of the house that he was scheming how to do it. I looked into his eyes and saw two demons, Pride and Fear. I tried to speak past the demons to the man and said, "You must do it His way." The man seemed profoundly insulted, and Pride answered, "I know that!" But he didn't know. I then saw Fear whisper: "Don't listen to him. He's a deceiver."

Then the Lord stepped beside me. As He did, I then saw Fear and Pride merge into one larger demon called Religion, and it declared: "Worship Him!" The man bowed low and wept upon the Lord's feet, declaring profuse love and praises. I knew that it was worship from this Religious spirit which Pride and Fear had merged to form. The worship was so demonstrative that it was repulsive. I then saw the word "*demon*strative."

I was amazed that the Lord did not seem to mind. He started to declare His love for the man, but before He could finish His sentence, this demon cried out, "I know you love me," and started quoting verses. The man then fell on the ground groveling in pretended religious ecstacy. The Lord then lovingly patted the man's head, knowing that He could not speak a word without the religious spirit interrupting Him.

I asked the Lord why He did not just cast this demon out. He replied, *"There is so little of the real man left*

238

that he would die. This kind can only come out with love." I thought of Jezebel in the church of Thyatira and what the Lord had said about her, **"I gave her time to repent…"** **(Revelation 2:21).** I then thought of Judas who had betrayed Him, yet he allowed him into His innermost circle of leaders. The Lord then said, *"I loved Judas, and My apostles learned love by having him with us. My own people delivered Me to the Romans, but I love them and I died for them too. When your love can win My brothers the Jews you can deliver any Judas and make him a Paul. You can win any Jezebel and make her a pure and holy bride. The religious people are your greatest enemies, but they are enemies for your sake. I desire for all to be saved, and only love can win the religious, so love you must if you will do My will. I rebuked Thyatira for tolerating Jezebel. You must not tolerate the evil, but you must love the people who are bound by it."*

Though I did not think it was possible, the Lord looked even more glorious than before. I was surprised that I could stand so close to such glory. He said, *"This is why the death of My people is so precious to Me. Those who seek to save their lives always lose them, but those who lose their lives for My sake will find true life. Now you know true life because you know love. Only by your death could you know this."*

I then looked at the house and all of those who composed it. Everything and everyone that I saw seemed to stir up this great feeling of love that was more wonderful than anything I had ever felt before. I wanted to go look at or talk to each one, but I did not want to leave the Lord's side Whose presence was even more compelling. Knowing my thoughts, he said, *"You need never fear leaving My side, because I have made My abode in you and I will be with you everywhere that you go."*

As I watched the presumptuous people, they were enjoying all of the blessings, and even thought of themselves as the reason for them, but they really were not even part of what was being built. Having just been one of them I also knew how shallow their enjoyment was, compared to what it could become, and a great compassion came over me for them. As I continued watching these people, they gradually become thinner in substance until they were just like the phantoms I had seen in the city that had been destroyed. Again I thought of the Lord's words, *"Those who seek to save their lives will always lose them, but those who lose their lives for My sake will find true life."*

I also watched as the Judas, going through his religious antics, turned so many people away from the house. Sometimes he would preach. Sometimes he would go into his fits of pretended ecstacy. I watched as those who focused on him too long would turn away. However, those who would look past him to the glory in the house would soon begin to see right through him as though he did not exist. This infuriated the demon in him, but it was powerless to do anything about it.

No Limits

Then I noticed that the building kept getting higher. The higher it grew the more glory it exuded and the further it could be seen. As a result, even more ships and people were coming through the storms, which although they were still raging, seemed unable to affect the island. As I wondered how high the building could get, the Lord turned to me and said, *"There is no limit to how high we can build this because I am the foundation and love is the cement."*

This caused me to look at the cement, which was transparent but radiated a great power. I wondered why I had not noticed this before; it was now so obvious and captivating. I then began to ponder how blind I had been to even the greatest wonders of this building until the Lord directed my attention to them. This caused me to turn back to the Lord and watch everything that He gave His attention to.

The Lord then began looking at the people who now composed the building. As I looked at them again I was immediately struck by the fact that they were *more* than people. I knew that they were the "new creation" that had transcended this creation, but now I saw how they had bridged the gap between the physical and spiritual realms, yet were clearly a part of both. They were unquestionably supernatural, which did not mean that they were not natural, but were far *more natural* than anything "natural" I had ever seen. They were more real than anything I had ever considered "real." They made everything else seem like a shadow.

Soon the glory that was coming from those who were a part of the building could be both seen and felt. The feeling was not like a touch, but like an emotion. As I walked close enough to this glory, it made me feel so good that I can only describe it is as a wonderful intoxication; not one that clouded the mind, but on the contrary, illuminated it. I felt somehow ennobled, not with pride, but with a powerful sense of destiny. I also felt a profound security, as if I were in complete harmony with the ground, the air, and especially the Lord and His house. This feeling was so good that I never wanted to move again.

With the addition of each new boat load of people, the transformation of those already a part of the building would continue, and the glory of the whole building would increase and expand. This made everyone in the building greatly rejoice with the coming of each new group of people.

Sharing The Glory

When those who came from the cemetery took their place in the building, those who were already a part tried to give the new their own glory. As they did this, the glory radiating from the Lord would increase, and He would give those who had given their own glory away, even more. Those who were the most devoted to this sharing would be the ones used to start the next level of the house, which kept going higher and higher.

I thought of how opposite this was from the jealousy which had before prevailed in the city. I then tried to ponder the jealousy to understand it more, but it was almost impossible to do. Because I could no longer feel jealousy I had a difficult time even understanding what it was—it seemed as unreal as if it had only existed in bad dreams. The joy of sharing was so great that not to do it now seemed incomprehensible. The more one shared his glory, the more he received to share.

This joy of sharing was so great that I knew that all of us would be spending eternity just seeking others with whom to share the glory. I then somehow knew that the Lord would be creating many new worlds just for us to have new places to share His glory. I understood that this was why He had created the universe with such diversity, and why He created it to continually expand. Those who touched His glory were touched by a love that had to share the glory, which caused them to expand. He had given us the universe with which to share His glory. He had set in motion a glorious chain reaction that would never stop! There were no limits on time or space, and we would need every bit of it!

As I looked at Jesus, I knew that He was the Wisdom of God. He was the Wisdom who would bring forth from his treasures things both old and new. He was the bridge between the old creation and the new, and He would forever be sharing both.

The Storms Return

Then suddenly my attention was turned toward the storms that had continued to grow in the sea. To my shock they had grown larger and faster than the house of the Lord, and were now coming toward the island.

Great waves covered the island and the building disappeared from my view, even though I was still very close to it. The fury of this storm was beyond comprehension, but I felt no fear at all. I knew that it was because I had already died to this world and had a life that could never be taken from me. Above all, I knew that I had His word. I stood on something that could not be overcome. As wonderful as the island had become, I was just as happy to die physically so that I would be free to carry the glory of the Lord to the rest of the universe that had so captured my attention. It really would have been hard to choose to stay or go, so I just rested and waited.

Gradually the storms abated and the building then re-emerged. Both the building and the island were much smaller, but were even more glorious. Then I noticed that the storms were just off shore and were returning. This happened several times, and each time the building would emerge it would be smaller, but more glorious. Each time that this happened the storms were also much smaller—they were wearing themselves out on the island. Soon the storms could only generate small waves that held no threat of any real damage. The glory of the house was now beyond any human description.

Then the clouds dissipated altogether into the most beautiful sky I had ever seen. As I gazed into the sky I began to realize that it was filled with the glory that was being emitted from the house. As I looked at the house I was amazed that there was no damage from the storm, though it was much smaller. Even so, the glory now coming from the house was much greater than before, and was reflected by everything. I felt that it was so great that it must already be extending far beyond the earth.

Then the vision changed and I was alone with the Lord. All of the great feelings were gone—even the love. He looked at me earnestly and said, *"The war is almost over. It is time to prepare for the storms. Tell My people that no one with His brother's blood on His hands will be used to build My house."*

I was trying hard to listen to these words in order to heed them, while still thinking about the great love I had felt. He then said, *"This was a dream, but it is real. You have known everything that I have shown you in this dream in your heart. Now believe with your heart and My love will be real to you again. This is your quest—to know My love."*

Comments

The general interpretation of this vision is obvious, but I do think that many of the feelings that I had during this experience are an important part of the message.

In looking at the different buildings which I knew represented denominations or movements, the architectural clash was so striking that it was grotesque. It was as if they were all so intent on being different that the most hideous skyline had been the result. I could not imagine anyone who happened upon such a city having any desire to enter it, even if the conflict had not been taking place.

The church is doing much more damage to herself through infighting than the enemies without are able to do. At that time I was consciously surprised that the Lord did not intervene in this destructive fighting. Those who were fighting against the other denominations, or movements, were all disqualified from being a part of the house which the Lord built.

This reminded me of King David, who, because he was a man of war and had shed blood" (I Chronicles 28:3) was not allowed to build the temple of the Lord. This did not disqualify David from salvation, or from being considered one of the great men of God of all time. I felt that many true saints, and even great men of God, were tragically disqualifying themselves from this most wonderful work of all by becoming embroiled in this spiritual civil war. This even caused them to lose the light that they had; only the peacemakers, and those who were trying to repair and build instead of tearing down, radiated with light in this vision.

I think that it was significant that almost all, if not all, of these buildings contained those who were true lights. These may appear as small lights now, but they will be the foundation upon which the Lord will build His house.

Because the sea sometimes represents "mass human-ity" in Scripture (see Revelation 17:18), the multitudes are going to rise up in great waves which will destroy much of the present, visible structure of the church. Those who are true lights were not swept away by the waves. Those who walk in truth have a foundation which cannot be shaken.

The Lord's command to release the sea did not cause the sea to rise up, but just removed that which was restraining it. The sea then came with fury against the island, as if it were being controlled by a great hatred. I believe this represented a great hatred against visible, institutional Christianity that will arise, and the Lord will allow it to destroy these institutions.

When these great tidal waves had stopped, there were no Christian institutions as represented by the buildings that men had constructed. However, all of the real Chris-tians remained. I do not think that it is wrong to keep trying to repair these structures, as the Lord honored and preserved those who did, but this vision affirmed deep within me the need to focus on building people, rather than trying to build another institution that will be able to stand in these times—none of them will stand.

Even though these buildings were destroyed, they each contained those who were to be pillars in His house. The house of the Lord was a brand new building, but those who became the main supports in it came from almost every denomination and movement. The Lord does have new wine to serve, but Isaiah 25:6 declares that the Lord will also serve "refined, aged wine." The

Lord will not use *either* the old or the new, but *both* the old and new.

The Lord's house was built in the midst of the increasing storms of rage and lawlessness. It radiated an even greater light because of those storms. I was encouraged that the Lord will build, on this earth, a church that really will reflect His glory, and that this age will not end until He does.

It could not be any other way. Moses contended when the Lord threatened to destroy Israel, that this would only leave the testimony that He could bring people out of Egypt, but could not lead them into the Promised Land. The Lord will have a testimony, through the church, that will last for all eternity. That testimony will be that He not only can forgive the sins of His church, but He also has the power and wisdom to deliver her from her sins, and to make her into a glorious bride without spot or wrinkle.

> **Now when Jesus came into the district of Ceasarea Philippi, He began asking His disciples, saying, "Who do people say that the Son of Man is?"**
>
> **And they said, "Some say John the baptist; and others, Elijah; but still others, Jeremiah, or one of the prophets."**
>
> **He said to them, *"But who do you say that I am?"***
>
> **And Simon Peter answered and said, "Thou art the Christ, the Son of the living God."**

And Jesus answered and said to him, "Blessed are you, Simon Barjona, *because flesh and blood did not reveal this to you, but My Father who is in heaven.*

And I also say to you that you are Peter, [a stone] and upon this rock [a large rock or bedrock] I will build my church; and the gates of Hades will not overpower it (Matthew 16:13-18).